THE BOOK OF RAIN

يد سعيد بن اوس الانصاري

ABŪ ZAYD SAʿĪD IBN AWS AL-ANṢĀRĪ

THE BOOK OF RAIN

WITH AN APPENDIX **ON THE NAMES OF THE WIND** BY IBN KHĀLAWAYH

TRANSLATED, WITH NOTES AND INTRODUCTION, BY DAVID LARSEN

WAVE BOOKS
SEATTLE/NEW YORK

PUBLISHED BY WAVE BOOKS

WWW.WAVEPOETRY.COM

WAVE BOOKS TITLES ARE DISTRIBUTED TO THE TRADE BY

CONSORTIUM BOOK SALES AND DISTRIBUTION

PHONE: 800-283-3572 / SAN 631-760X

LIBRARY OF CONGRESS CATALOGING-IN-PUBLICATION DATA

NAMES: ABŪ ZAYD AL-ANṢARĪ, SAʿĪD IBN AWS, -830 AUTHOR

LARSEN, DAVID, 1970- TRANSLATOR

TITLE: THE BOOK OF RAIN / ABŪ ZAYD SAʿĪD IBN AWS AL-ANṢĀRĪ;

TRANSLATED, WITH NOTES AND INTRODUCTION, BY DAVID LARSEN

OTHER TITLES: KITĀB AL-MAṬAR.

DESCRIPTION: FIRST EDITION | SEATTLE : WAVE BOOKS, 2025.

IDENTIFIERS: LCCN 2025008136 | ISBN 9798891060364 PAPERBACK

SUBJECTS: LCSH: RAIN AND RAINFALL—EARLY WORKS TO 1800

ARABIC LANGUAGE—GLOSSARIES, VOCABULARIES, ETC.—EARLY WORKS

TO 1800 | CYAC: MANUSCRIPTS, ARABIC—EARLY WORKS TO 1800.

CLASSIFICATION: LCC QC859 .A1813 2025 | DDC 551.503—DC23/ENG/20250617

LC RECORD AVAILABLE AT HTTPS://LCCN.LOC.GOV/2025008136

DESIGNED BY CRISIS

PRINTED IN THE UNITED STATES OF AMERICA

9 8 7 6 5 4 3 2 1

FIRST EDITION

SOME TRANSLATIONS AND RESEARCH IN THIS VOLUME

APPEARED PREVIOUSLY IN *DEAR KATHLEEN: ESSAYS ON*

THE OCCASION OF KATHLEEN FRASER'S 80TH BIRTHDAY,

THE JOURNAL *POSTMEDIEVAL*, AND *LIGHTNING-SCENES*

(WAVE PAMPHLET NO. 10). THANKS TO THE EDITORS.

ABBREVIATIONS AND SYMBOLS

art.	article
b.	*ibn* (son of)
bt.	*bint* (daughter of)
ca.	circa
cf.	compare
fol.	folio
d.	death date
K.	*Kitāb* (Book of)
√	linguistic root
MS	manuscript
pl.	plural
sg.	singular

Aghānī	*Kitāb al-Aghānī* (The Book of Songs) by Abū l-Faraj al-Iṣbahānī, d. 356/967
Lisān	*Lisān al-ʿarab* (The Tongue of the Arabs) by Jamāl al-Dīn ibn Manẓūr, d. 711/1312
Shiʿr	*Al-Shiʿr wa-l-shuʿarāʾ* (Poetry and Poets) by Ibn Qutayba, d. 276/889

Years are given by Hijrī and Gregorian dates (in that order), separated by a forward slash.

All material between [square brackets] is the translator's insertion.

INTRODUCTION

The contents of the future are the contents of a cloud. If this statement has poetic truth, it owes to a part-to-whole relationship between weather and experience generally. The course of a day is so permeated by its weather that the presence or absence of clouds is a natural synecdoche for all the day might hold. This is as true of clouds seen from a distance, which affect us as predictive signs, as it is of clouds overhead.

Rain too can be a synecdoche for the affecting circumstances of any moment, and equally a metaphor. Philology backs this up: Latin *casus* "fallen" supplies most European languages with their words for "the case," except German and Swedish where it's called the *Fall*. So too in Arabic the active participle of *waqaʿa* "to fall" is used for what is "actually occurring" (*wāqiʿ*). And when God makes something happen, He "sends it down" (*anzalahu*). In English we find this idiom in what "befalls" us, and things that take place are popularly said to "go down." "Coming down," meanwhile, has an apocalyptic ring in modern English, as in the Beatles' "Helter Skelter" (1968), deriving just the same from the down-coming rain.

In lived experience, rain is an emotional coefficient to all things. To ask whether rain will fall on a given day is the world's least shallow question. It is the mocker and consoler of every feeling, and the complicator of every outdoor plan.

♦

No rivers flow into the Arabian Peninsula. Before desalinization technology, all its fresh water originated from the sky. Great tracts of the peninsula were inhabitable only at rain-seasonal intervals, and have until modern times been the exclusive territory of pastoral-nomadic communities. That these communities would develop an elaborate vocabulary for precipitation and groundwater is unsurprising, and yet (cautioned by the fallacy of "Eskimo Words for Snow") I refrain from supposing a causal link.[1] The proliferation of Arabic words for weather is proportionate to the proliferation of Arabic words for all kinds of things.

Right away it should be acknowledged that the *Book of Rain* is not a definitive list. More exhaustive catalogues of Arabic weather-words are out there, as for example *Kitāb al-Azmina wa-l-amkina* (The Book of Seasons and Places) of al-Marzūqī (d. 421/1030). The *Book of Rain*'s distinction is that it is the earliest known to have been made. In fact, it unites two catalogues under one title: *K. al-Maṭar* (The Book of Rain) and *K. al-Miyāh* (The Book of Waters). The combination is only natural, as the life-giving work of rain is done mostly in the form of groundwater.

Rain gives life, and for this reason the beneficial raincloud is called *al-Ḥayā* "The Life-Giver." But to those who live exposed to it, rain is to be dreaded as much as wished for. This is attested throughout the Qur'ān, where *maṭar* "rain" is mostly punitive; for benevolent rains, the word *ghayth* is used.[2] It happens that the magnum opus of Imru' al-Qays (d. ca. 550 CE) ends with this description of a destructive rainstorm:

> "Companion, do you see the lightning whose flicker I am showing you,
> like fluorescent hands [at play] in the crowned and mounded clouds?
> The lightning's glare gives light—or are those lamps belonging to a monk
> who causes oil to ride the twisted wicks?"
> With my friends I sat waiting on it, between Ḍārij
> and al-ʿUdhayb, I gave the skies a scanning.

The north side of its flood gripped Qaṭan, we surmised,
    and Yadhbul and al-Sattār were on its south.
Then, in the territory of Kuthayfa, it let its water go,
    replanting thorn trees head downward.
The violence of its disgorge, when it passed over al-Qanān,
    drove pied goats down from every hillside refuge.
Taymā' lost its palms. Not a trunk was left standing,
    nor any structure made from aught but stone.
Mt. Thabīr came under its snout. The mudslides
    of the storm left it striped like a grandee's poncho.
It dressed the top of Mt. Mujaymir in a blurry coat of flotsam,
    looking in the light of dawn like a spindle's whirl.
And in the desert of Ghabīṭ it spread its wares
    like the Yemeni arriving with his heavy load.
At sunup, the birds of Jiwā' tittered
    as if they'd hailed the dawn with peppered wine.
By nightfall, the carcasses of Jiwā''s drowned beasts
    poked up like bulbs of onion along the valley margin.[3]

In the third verse from the end, it helps to know that "the Yemeni" is a traveling clothes-merchant, whose colorful wares are a simile for wildflowers that bloom after a storm. Given its combination of fecundating and destructive powers, rain is an unavoidable figure for *jouissance*. And so the beloved's charms are relished like a rain-fed meadow—or the water of the rain itself, as in the poem by al-Ḥādira (late sixth century CE):

In conversation, you're struck by her beauty,
    and how nice it would be to join lips with her smile,
like sipping rainwater, after the East Wind taps a night-flying cloud,
    and the sediment sinks away in the pool's sweet stillness.

Streambeds are caught off guard by the storm's scouring,
but their flow clears up after the rains die down.
Their water is the streamlets' plaything, before it goes
dividing into shares among the roots of soft green plants.[4]

At this intersection of *eros* and inundation, the poetic valences of rain are nowhere near exhausted. To list them here is not my plan, but early Arabic poetry—the primary evidentiary resource for generations of lexicographers—is a good place to start. The *Book of Rain* is a work of lexicography, and a pioneering one at that, even if the genre it represents did not stay viable for long.

♦

Pride of place in Arabic lexicography has always gone to the lemmatized dictionary, beginning with *K. al-ʿAyn* (The Book of the Letter *ʿAyn*) of al-Khalīl b. Aḥmad (d. ca. 170/786) who was one of Abū Zayd al-Anṣārī's teachers. But dictionaries were not the only genre of lexicographical writing, nor even the mainstream norm until long after. Over Islam's second and third centuries, dictionaries were outnumbered by lexica in which words are grouped by theme rather than alphabetic makeup. These themes were drawn from the basic conditions of traditional Bedouin life, as represented in an outpouring of treatises listing all the Arabic names for domestic and wild animals, the seasons and the months, the hours of the day and night, and other fundaments of desert life. At least ten different scholars (including Abū Zayd) produced works with the title *K. al-Farq* (Book of Comparative Anatomy), nor were there fewer than five *K. al-Silāḥ* (Books of Weapons), three *K. al-Nakhl* (Books of the Date Palm), etc. Of these texts, some are little more than word-lists, and some are more discursive. Nearly all of them feature poetry. The majority have not survived, and in this regard Abū Zayd was comparatively well-favored: of some forty-five attested titles, six are extant, including the *Book of Rain* and *Book of Waters*.

What's interesting from the standpoint of media history is that none of these books are traceable to written marks made by Abū Zayd. Notes and *aides-mémoire* he no doubt kept, but the end-products of his intellectual labor were recited lectures for his hearers to memorize and pass on. So it is that his books speak from a primarily-oral knowledge culture, in which audition (*samāʿ*) was the default pedagogical channel, presenting as *lectures put into writing* by his students, his students' students, and so on. They are prefaced not by an author's introduction, but a transmission statement, enumerating the chain of authorities through whom the text was passed. Sometimes, writers indicate that their version of the text was authenticated by a senior scholar, declaring: "I read it out to him" (*Qaraʾtuhu ʿalayhi*), that is, "I recited the text out loud for his approval."

In the long, collaborative process through which books were produced in the second and third centuries of Islam, the distinction between author and transmitter is hard to make with confidence. "During this period," writes Gregor Schoeler, "transmitters were very much involved in shaping a text. They supplemented the material, shortened or reworked it."[5] Who, then, is the true author of the *Book of Rain*? Abū Zayd who told it out loud, or the men who wrote it down?[6] For the *Book of Rain*, there are comparative grounds for affirming Abū Zayd's authorship: one need only look to his *K. al-Nawādir fī l-lugha* (Book of Lexical Rarities), which (as described ahead) was swollen with supplementary material by generations of later scholars. In the *Book of Rain*, these latter-day interpolations are not in evidence. The apparent aim of its transmitters and copyists was to preserve the simulacrum of a lecture by Abū Zayd. Far be it from me to scuttle their labors! It is much more fun to perpetuate the illusion than to destabilize it, and in that spirit I am pleased to give out the *Book of Rain* under Abū Zayd Saʿīd b. Aws al-Anṣārī's good name.

Audition endured as a pedagogical medium well after Abū Zayd's day. Lexical monography, by contrast, had a fourth-/tenth-century endpoint. Treatise-length word-lists were by then antiquated vehicles for philological research, and with the absorption of their contents into ever more compendious and easily-browsed works, some thematic monographs were recopied but few new ones were produced until the Mamluk period, which saw a revival of the form. The Abbasid-era examples that survive are a small fraction of the total output, and their preservation probably owes more to academic nostalgia than scholarly utility.

Then again, the utility of these texts was all along predicated on nostalgia for the imagined purity of the Arabic language. As treated by the early scholars under the rubric of *Mā talḥanu fī-hi l-ʿāmma* (Vulgar Dialecticisms), the differences between literary-grade discourse and the everyday *parole* of Abbasid Iraq were glaring. For Arabic *langue* worthy of study, there were two funds of evidence. One was historical precedent, as enshrined in proverbial expressions, pre-Islamic poetry, the text of the Qurʾān and, to a lesser extent, Prophetic hadith. The other was contemporary Bedouin speech. Certain tribes' supposed immunity to linguistic corruption gave their dialects a classical authority that was tantamount to the ancients'.[7] Abū Zayd's personal standards are a matter of record: "I do not attribute any word or phrase to 'the Arabs,'" he said, "unless I have heard it from a member of Bakr b. Hawāzin, the Banū Kilāb, or the Banū Hilāl, or from the high-dwelling lowlanders or the low-dwelling highlanders."[8] Both halves of this statement point to the western part of the Najd (the Arabian Peninsula's north-central plateau), where by his own account Abū Zayd spent time interviewing native speakers.[9]

All these population groups belong to Qays, who are invoked in the *Book of Rain*'s first sentence: "The tribesmen of Qays say. . . ." Qays were identified with the "northern Arabs" whose occupation of West and Central Arabia predated the Late Antique incursion of "southern Arabs" from Yemen. Among the latter was Abū Zayd's ancestral tribe of Khazraj, who arrived in Yathrib (the future

Medina) during this period of migration. It was, in other words, not the dialect of his own tribal forebears that Abū Zayd sought out, but the dialects of other groups.

No group was without phonological idiosyncrasies. Bakr and the rest of Hawāzin had the habit of *kaskasa* (pronouncing the second singular pronouns *-ka* and *-ki* with a final /*s*/), and Tamīm spoke with *taltala* (voweling present-tense verb prefixes with /*i*/ instead of /*a*/).[10] And some peculiarities of ʿAnbarī dialect are mentioned in the *Book of Rain*. Some of these tribes could even point to occurrences of their dialect in the Qurʾān—for example, Hawāzin at *Sūrat al-Raʿd* (Thunder) 13:31.[11] Their departures from koine were part of what made these dialects exemplary.

The ideological utility of exemplary dialects is easy to understand. "[P]roviding the urban scholar with the necessary material to promote the myth of the *ʿarabiyya*, the pure and idealized form of Arabic alleged to have been spoken by the Bedouin and in which, as dogma had it, Muḥammad delivered the revelation," Bedouin dialect legitimated Arabophone hegemony by serving as a representative paradigm.[12] What is more, living speakers were a renewable resource for the scholar in a way that reports of the past were not.

The core status of Bedouin speech within Arabic linguistic inquiry may be the one thing early scholars agreed on. The literary results of their work are an aggregation of cultural material too complex and lively to be a planned construction, as may be appreciated in the works of language scholarship whose recitation began in Abū Zayd's day.

♦

"Abū Zayd's day" is less aptly spoken of than his *century*, as his reputed age at death was ninety five years. Most of them were spent in Basra (a cultural center of Iraq well before the capital was established at Baghdad), but his expertise and ancestry were of an Arabia long since claimed by the past. Abū Zayd was third in a line of scholars that began with his grandfather Zayd b. Thābit (d. ca. 45/666), the famous "scribe of the revelation" (*kātib al-wāḥy*) who was secretary to the Prophet Muḥammad and an editor of the Qur'ān after the Prophet's death.[13] There being more than one companion of the Prophet called "Abū Zayd al-Anṣārī," our author is in some contexts prone to overshadow. His persona was never incorporated into tales or legends (as happened to more than one grammarian), and reports of his table talk aren't many. Biographical facts say a lot, though, like his willingness to visit Kufa, where much of his *Book of Lexical Rarities* was gleaned from recitations by al-Mufaḍḍal al-Ḍabbī (d. 170/786-7); among his Basran contemporaries Abū Zayd seems to be the only one to have made the short trip.[14] Coupled with this freedom from regional chauvinism was his lack of habituation to courtly life, whether by ascetic disinclination or, as has been suggested, a want of entertainment value in his scholarship.[15] No participant in sectarian controversy, he is nevertheless identified with the freethinking theological school of the Muʿtazila, and his teacher ʿAmr b. ʿUbayd (d. 144/761) was an early principal of the movement.[16]

These commitments are unengaged in Abū Zayd's scholarly work. Nor do his books reflect the jovial demeanor that shines through in reports—like his habit of awarding nicknames to his students, reported in *Marātib al-naḥwiyyīn* (Echelons of the Grammarians) by Abū l-Ṭayyib al-Lughawī (d. 351/962):

> Abū Zayd's character was agreeable and affectionate. We are informed by Muḥammad b. Yaḥyā (al Ṣūlī, d. 335/946) that Muḥammad b. Yazīd (al-Mubarrad, d. 286/900) said:
>
> Abū Zayd used to give people nicknames. Al-Jarmī (d. 225/839) he called *al-Kalb* "The Dog," for his bloodshot eyes and combative nature. Al-Māzinī (d. ca. 247/861) he called *Tudruj* "The Pheasant," for his funny way of walking. Abū Ḥātim [al-Sijistānī] he called *Ra's al-Baghl* "Mule Head," for his head's great size. Al-Tawwazī

(d. 230/844 or 238/852) he called *Abū l-Wazwāz* "Father of the Cicada" for his nimbleness and alacrity of wit. And al-Ziyādī (d. 249/863) he called *Ṭāriq* "Night Caller" for his habit of visiting Abū Zayd after dark.[17]

Nor did Abū Zayd exempt himself from mirth. "I stopped in at a butcher who was selling paunch," he is said to have said, "and [using a dual form seldom heard in vernacular speech] I asked: 'Boy, how much for paunches twain?' He said: 'Dirhams twain, thou bore!'"[18] Jocular Arabic literature abounds in tales like these, where grammarians try to communicate with ordinary people and fail.[19] If the report may be believed, Abū Zayd was happy to tell these stories on himself.

Abū Zayd's students include his century's most eminent grammarian (Sībawayh, d. ca. 180/796), poet (Abū Nuwās, d. ca. 200/815), and prose writer (al-Jāḥiẓ, d. 255/869).[20] As an authority on grammar, he was highly esteemed, but it is as a lexicographer that he is remembered. "Abū Zayd said" is a refrain throughout dictionaries that are still in regular use. Of his surviving books, all are works of lexicography, and all have been edited for print:

1. *Kitāb al-Shajar wa-l-kalāʾ* (The Book of Trees and Herbage) is a text of some importance to the history of botanical science. Of the early Arabic "books of plants" (*kutub al-nabāt*), Abū Zayd's is the first to be organized along classificatory lines—chiefly, the categorical distinction enforced in its title.[21] The word *shajar* was classically applicable to "plants" in general, but Abū Zayd uses it in counterpoise to *kalāʾ*, which is a pastoral word for "grazing plants." Along this line, his book separates plants into genera, which it treats in separate sections. Palms and cereal crops are mentioned in neither category.

K. al-Shajar wa-l-kalāʾ reaches us in the version of al-Ḥusayn b. Aḥmad b. Khālawayh (d. 371/980-1). Ibn Khālawayh's preface states that he had read out several of Abū Zayd's books for the approval of Abū ʿUmar al-Zāhid (Ghulām

Thaʿlab, d. 345/967), who knew them from his master Thaʿlab (d. 291/904), who knew them from Ibn Najda (mid-third/mid-ninth century).[22] Aside from Ibn Najda, these are all well-known scholars, who assembled to propagate Abū Zayd's books for over a century after his death, while producing their own works of original scholarship.[23]

2. *Kitāb al-Libāʾ wa-l-laban* (The Book of Beestings and Milk) is a short list of names for the ways that milk can abound with cream or lack it, smell sweet or sour, turn rancid, turn into cheese, etc. Though goats and sheep are mentioned, it is mostly about the milk of camels. (*Beestings* is an old Teutonic word for the first milk drawn from an animal just delivered of its firstborn, and this is the meaning of *libāʾ*.)

K. al-Libāʾ wa-l-laban was set down by Abū Saʿīd al-Sukkarī (d. 275/888) from independent versions by Abū Ḥātim al-Sijistānī and Abū l-Faḍl al-Riyāshī (d. 257/869), both of whom heard it directly from Abū Zayd. Editorial comment by Abū Ḥātim and Abū l-Faḍl is incorporated piecemeal within the text (just as commentary by Ibn Khālawayh occurs in the text of *K. al-Shajar wa-l-kalāʾ*). This never happens in the *Book of Rain*, where every word is notionally Abū Zayd's.

3. *Kitāb al-Nawādir fī l-lugha* (The Book of Lexical Rarities) stands out from Abū Zayd's other books in many respects. Heaped with supplementary material by its transmitters, it is the longest of his extant works by far. It is also the only one built around poetic testimonia, well over a thousand verses. (The *Book of Rain*, by contrast, contains just twenty-six.) In fact *K. al-Nawādir* may be described as a book of poetic commentary first and a lexicon second.[24] Words are its subject insofar as they depart from norms and are heard in rare verses and proverbial expressions.

It was written down by al-Akhfash the Younger (Abū l-Ḥasan ʿAlī, d. 315/927), who heard it from al-Mubarrad and al-Sukkarī, both of whom had heard it from

Abū Ḥātim plus one other source (al-Mubarrad from al-Tawwazī, al-Sukkarī from al-Riyāshī). All six are quoted throughout the book, as are numerous reports by al-Aṣmaʿī (d. 213/828) and Abū ʿUbayda (d. 209/824–5), who were Abū Zayd's contemporaries among the grammarians of Basra.

4. *Kitāb Masāʾiya* (The Book of Vitiated Qualities) was preserved as an appendix to the *Book of Lexical Rarities*. In one place, al-Akhfash says that al-Mubarrad did not know *K. Masāʾiya*, which means the book came to him through al-Sukkarī alone. That it was originally an independent work is made clear in his statement on the last page of *K. al-Nawādir*: "This concludes *K. al-Nawādir* and the addition of *K. Masāʾiya* that was made to it, with praise and thanks to God."[25]

It truly is a book of qualities, and not social types. Nor is it a book of disabilities belonging to the genre of *kutub al-ʿāhāt*, like al-Jāḥiẓ's *K. al-Burṣān wa-l-ʿurjān wa-l-ʿumyān wa-l-ḥūlān* (The Book of Lepers, the Lame, the Blind, and the Cross-Eyed), although many of the qualities defined in it are beyond the subject's power to control (such as left-handedness, speech impediments, and ungainly body types). These appear alongside expressions for ethical flaws (sloth, cowardice) and moral abuses (voyeurism, parasitism). Nonhuman faults are included too, in expressions for unworthy vessels, worn-out clothes, and worthless livestock. And some positive traits are also mentioned.

5. *Kitāb al-Hamz* (The Book of *Hamza*) is a list of Arabic words in which the glottal stop called *hamza* (ء) features as a root letter. Of Abū Zayd's extant works it is the only one with alphabetic order: words are grouped into chapters by the first consonant in each root, or the second consonant when first position is occupied by *hamza* itself. There is no discussion of phonology or prefatory matter of any kind. If words with *hamza* have anything else in common, Abū Zayd doesn't mention it.

K. al-Hamz was transmitted by the same uncle-nephew chain that preserved the *Book of Rain*, who were second- and third-generation descendants of the grammarian Abū Muḥammad Yaḥyā b. al-Mubārak al-Yazīdī (d. 202/818). Abū Muḥammad had the same Basran teachers as Abū Zayd, and went on to serve Hārūn al-Rashīd (r. 170–193/786–809) as court tutor, spending the rest of his life under caliphal patronage. He is best remembered for the number of his descendants who carried on the Yazīdī name in the literary sciences: six sons and fifteen grandsons, among them Abū Jaʿfar Aḥmad b. Muḥammad al-Yazīdī (d. before 260/874). According to transmission statements in the *Book of Rain* and *Book of Hamza*, Abū Jaʿfar heard both books directly from Abū Zayd, and taught them to his fraternal nephew Abū ʿAbd Allāh Muḥammad (d. 310/922). Himself a tutor to the caliph's court, Abū ʿAbd Allāh put together some still-extant poetry collections (including the *dīwān* of al-Ḥādira quoted above) and compiled a history of his family (*K. Akhbār al-Yazīdiyyīn*), now lost.[26] Without him, we would not have the *Book of Rain*.

Abū Zayd's vanished works are many. The *Fihrist* (Bibliography) of Ibn al-Nadīm (d. ca. 385/995) lists more than two dozen:

Aymān ʿaymān[27]	Bereft and Wanting
Ḥīla wa-maḥāla[28]	Power and Agency
al-Qaws wa-l-turs[29]	Bow and Shield
al-Miʿzā[30]	Goats
al-Ibil wa-l-shāʾ	Camels and Sheep
al-Abyāt	Verses [of Obscure and Ambiguous Meanings]
Khalq al-insān	Human Anatomy
al-Gharāʾiz[31]	Character Traits
al-Lughāt	Arabic Dialects
Qirāʾat Abī ʿAmr	Abū ʿAmr's Reading of the Qurʾān[32]
al-Jamʿ wa-l-tathniya	The Plural and the Dual
Buyūtāt al-ʿarab	Aristocratic Families of the Arabs

Takhfīf al-hamza[33]	Elision of the *Hamza*
al-Khubʾa[34]	The Daughter
al-Muqtaḍab	Apocope
al-Wuḥūsh	Wild Animals
al-Farq	Comparative Anatomy
Faʿaltu wa-afʿaltu	Ist- and IVth-form Verbs
Gharīb al-asmāʾ	Uncommon Nouns
al-Maṣādir	Verbal Nouns
al-Jilsa[35]	The Seat
Nābih wa-nabīh	Gentle and Genteel
al-Wāḥid	The Singular
al-Tamr	The Fruit of the Date Palm
Naʿt al-mushāfihāt	Characteristics of Oral Communications
al-Manṭiq	*Logos* (?)

The following titles can additionally be gleaned from bio-bibliographical literature at large:

al-Iʿrāb	Desinential Syntax
al-Amthāl[36]	Proverbial Expressions
al-Barrī wa-l-khazāʾim	Nose Rings
al-Taḍārub	Difference of Opinion
al-Jawd wa-l-bukhl	Generosity and Parsimony
al-Raḥl wa-l-qatab	Saddle and Hump
al-Suʾdud	Leadership Qualities
al-Ṣifāt	Characteristics [of Various Things]
Gharīb al-ḥadīth	Uncommon Vocabulary in Prophetic Hadith
al-Lāmāt	Uses of the Letter *Lām*
Lughāt al-Qurʾān[37]	Arabic Dialects Occurring in the Qurʾān
al-Muthallath/al-Tathlīth	Verbs with Three Different Vowelings

Maʿānī l-Qurʾān	Themes of the Qurʾān
al-Maktūm	What Is Hidden (?)
al-Naḥw al-kabīr	A Large Grammar
al-Hashāsha wa-l-bashāsha	Gaiety and Cheer
al-Ward	The Rose (?)

Many of these titles demonstrate Abū Zayd's attention to finer points of Arabic morphology and semantics. *K. Nābih wa-nabīh*, for example, was probably about participial and adjectival forms with the same meaning. Some thematic titles may have been excerpted chapters from his *K. al-Ṣifāt*, which (judging from other works with that title) was a multithematic glossary.[38] This would explain the *Book of Nose Rings*, which cannot have filled many pages.

There seems no way to date these works relative to one another. Abū Zayd's career is indivisible into periods. In Basra he was born, and in Basra he remained a bachelor to the end of his days. In his later years, we are told that his memory failed him, but not his good humor. It was then that al-Riyāshī approached Abū Zayd with a manuscript copy of the *Book of Trees and Herbage*, in order that his aged teacher might authenticate its contents. "May I read it out to you?" he asked.

"Don't bother," said Abū Zayd. "I've already forgotten it."[39]

♦

Does the *Book of Rain* count as natural history, or is it a book of language only? The answer depends on your expectations of natural history as a literary genre. In early modern Europe, natural history's emergence is identified with the purge of folkloric material from inquiry into plant and animal life. A rededication of language to nonlinguistic knowledge is how Michel Foucault characterized it, saying that natural history "exists as a task only in so far as things and language happen to be separate."[40] This obviously excludes the *Book of Rain*, whose sources are purely linguistic. The book is devoid of reference to any particulars of the kind that make up a *historia*, that is, a systematic collection of observations of the world.[41] No datable event is recorded in it—not one drought, battle, pilgrimage, flood, or anything that climate scientists might use in the way Nilometer readings have been correlated with the Medieval Warm Period,[42] or records of French grape harvests with the Little Ice Age that followed.[43] I don't like to discount the *Book of Rain*'s utility for climate science, but it is not a work of empiricism, and the case for calling it a natural history is difficult to sustain.

This does not exempt the *Book of Rain* from the history of science. Writing of the *Book of Trees and Herbage*, Thomas Bauer names Abū Zayd as the first Arabic lexicographer to submit colloquial Bedouin plant-names to botanical classification in a semi-systematic fashion.[44] The gaps and shortcomings in his method are for Bauer symptomatic of "a clash between the desire to explain time-honored Arab concepts in their original, prescientific meanings, and the desire to create a logical system."[45]

In the *Book of Rain*, we find a similar tension between epistemic imperatives. Different principles of categorization are at work from section to section, and sequence is variously determined. In one passage (ahead at note lxxxi), Abū Zayd treats four words for water in the order of their mention in a Qurʾānic verse. Other passages present a "braiding" effect where two strands of word-meanings alternate in an ABAB pattern. The practical advantage of this alternation is not obvious, but the same pattern is at work in lexica of later centuries, such as *K. al-Mukhaṣṣaṣ* (The Book of Specialized Vocabulary) of Ibn Sīdah (d. 458/1066).

In the *Book of Rain*'s first section, sequence is determined by astrological and seasonal patterns. There follow a series of rains organized by relative fineness, after which the rains are qualified by duration, volume and aftereffects in no clear order. Coming last are two names for rain in general and two words for rain seen falling from a distance—and here the ABAB pattern is shown off admirably:

> *Al-ghayth* is a name for rain in general. *Al-sabal* "The Trailing Garment" is rain that hangs between cloud and earth, from the point of its leaving the cloud to its impact on the ground. A rain of little breadth may be called *al-saḥāba* "a cloud," whether its drops are few or many, much like *al-shuʾbūb* "The Cloudburst." Similar to *al-sabal* are *al-ʿathānīn* "The Chin Hairs," which is another name for rain [that dangles] between cloud and earth.

Typologies like these are on the outside margins of scientific genera, and plenty of other expectations of meteorology go unmet by the *Book of Rain* besides. With that, a side-word is in order, showing how far the scientific thinkers of Abū Zayd's century went into these questions, and to what degree Greek science supplied their terms and guided their thinking. Take for instance the doctrine of equilibrium between the opposed qualities of hot and cold and wet and dry.[46] The meteorological writings attributed to the second/eighth-century alchemist Jābir b. Ḥayyān attest to its naturalization within Islamic science, as in his *K. al-Ikhrāj mā fī l-quwwat ilā l-fiʿl* (The Book of Actualizing What Abides in Potentiality):

> Thunder, lightning, winds, earthquakes, rains, and all other such events are consequent upon the four elements. Clouds, for example, result from the vertical accumulation of vapor, of which there are two kinds: moist and dry. When hot, moist vapor ascends to a certain height, it starts to coagulate, and if its moisture is very great then it travels back down in the form of rain, leaving the nimbus undissolved; this is where rain comes from. The coagulation of water also takes place in the event of reduced moisture and colder air, these variables determining the size [of its droplets] and the force with which water is displaced from the air. And when heat and moisture are balanced, the vapor coagulates into a nimbus without producing rain at all.[47]

The insight that warm air holds more moisture than cold air may be traced to Aristotle's *Meteorology*, which first entered Arabic in the flawed version of Yaḥyā b. al-Biṭrīq (d. ca. 215/830).[48] In Islamic scientific tradition, the influence of Aristotle's *Meteorology* was surpassed by the *Meteorology* of his student Theophrastus

(d. 288 BCE)—a text that has disappeared in Greek, but survives in its Arabic translation by Ibn al-Khammār (d. ca. 421/1030).[49]

The texts of Yaʿqūb b. Isḥāq al-Kindī (d. ca. 252/866) show that Theophrastus's reception in Arabic went back centuries further.[50] Best remembered as a philosopher, al-Kindī wrote on a variety of scientific and technical themes, including astrology, cryptography, and the manufacture of swords. His treatise *Fī l-ʿilla allatī li-hā takūnu baʿḍ al-mawāḍiʿ lā takādu tumṭaru* (On the cause for which some places are scarcely rained on) discards Aristotle's chimerical notion of the wind as a "dry evaporation" rising vertically from the earth and then sent into lateral motion by heaven's rotation (*Meteorology* II.4), and embraces the Theophrastean principle of horror vacui. Modern meteorology is still in agreement with Theophrastus as channeled by al-Kindī in the matter of high- and low-pressure systems, and the winds they generate:

> All bodies undergo contraction when chilled, after which they take up less space than they occupied before their chilling. When heated, they undergo expansion, and take up more space than they occupied before their heating. Thus does air flow from a hot, expanded location toward one that is cold and contracted, and this flow is what we call the wind—for we give the name of "wind" (*rīḥ*) to the flow of air and "wave" (*mawj*) to the flow of water.[51]

There is no such science to be found in Abū Zayd's book. But if the *Book of Rain* excludes materialist causality, it also excludes superstition and religious beliefs. In order to appreciate this, it is important not to miss this marginal note on fol. 6v of the unique manuscript of the *Book of Rain*, apposite to the Names of Thunder:

> Abū Zayd informed us on the authority of ʿAmr b. ʿUbayd, on the authority of al-Ḥasan [al-Baṣrī], that the Prophet said: "Thunder is the angel in charge of clouds, and when you hear its voice, it is praising God."

The hadith is discussed ahead in note xxviii (page 38). Here what's most significant is that it was written in the margin, meaning that Abū Zayd did *not* enter it into the *Book of Rain*.[52]

The book's lack of devotional content is consistent with its mission, into which the causes of coming-to-be and passing-away don't enter. But it is still relevant to History of Science, especially the opening section where the archaic astrological system of *anwāʾ* "asterisms" is schematized. Asterisms are small constellations (some consisting of single stars) seen just above the eastern horizon at the break of dawn. On the alternation of these stars was based a native calendar whose pre-Islamic function was to assist in prayers for rain.[53] In surviving accounts, the *anwāʾ* are divested of pagan associations, surviving as an astral almanac of the kind called a *parapēgma*.[54] As presented in the *Book of Rain*, they form a calendar for periodizing rainfall only. They predict nothing, nor are they credited with causal powers, nor is there any claim that phenomena occurring during a given asterism are predictive of anything else—although there are many folkloric instances of this in Islam, as where al-Jāḥiẓ says of the Kaʿba: "If the door facing Iraq is struck by rain, then Iraq will have rainfall and fecundity that year. If the side facing Syria is struck, then Syria will have rainfall and fecundity that year. And if rain strikes the House on all its sides, the rainfall and fecundity will be general."[55]

Nor does prognostication of rain from clouds enter much into the *Book of Rain*, which tells that *al-Ḥayā* is "abundant rain," but not how to recognize the cloud that brings it. Two generations later, Ibn Qutayba (d. 276/889) took more of a phenomenological approach in *al-Anwāʾ fī mawāsim al-ʿarab* (Asterisms in the Seasonal Observances of the Arabs), 175:

> When the white part of a cloud is tinged with red, that is a sign that it brings no water, and a sign of drought. A verse by al-Nābigha al-Dhubyānī (late sixth century CE) speaks of clouds that

cover the flank of Mt. Tīn with their red-tinged shadow,
bringing on cold haze with little water in it.[56]

There was also a literary subgenre of prose anecdote called *waṣf al-maṭar* "description of the rain," in which mastery of Arabic weather vocabulary is shown to make predictions possible. The lexicographer Ibn Durayd (d. 321/933) produced an entire book with this title: thirty short reports featuring colorful prose descriptions of rain and clouds and pasturelands, each followed by a glossary. Not all involve prognosis of the weather, but this one does:

> Abū Ḥātim related to us that al-Aṣmaʿī said: After [the pre-Islamic poet] Muʿaqqir b. Ḥimār al-Bāriqī had lost his sight, he went out one day, led by his daughter. On hearing thunder, he asked her: "What do you see?" She said: "The cloud I see is the color of dark clay (*ḥammāʾ*), furrowed like the placenta of a she-camel with a sagging girth, her chest dipping low to the ground."
>
> "Not bad!" Muʿaqqir said. Hearing more thunder, he asked again: "What do you see?" She said: "To me, the cloud looks a rotten piece of meat, half of it firm and half rent open." And he said: "Shelter me beneath a myrrh. Protection from heavy rain is what myrrh trees do best!"
>
> Ibn Durayd said: *Al-ḥammāʾ* is the color black tinged with red. The "furrows" in the cloud are created by lightning. The "placenta" (*al-ḥiwalāʾ*) is a fine membrane which falls out along with the camel's newborn; the simile suggests that the cloud was "pregnant" with a large quantity of water.[57]

In this kind of weather report, the forecast is more of a narrative premise than a practical application of vocabulary.[58] But practical applications can be envisioned, as where the legal scholar al-Shāfiʿī (d. 204/820) observes that in order to face the Kaʿba, faraway worshippers must calculate their position relative to Mecca using such markers as the stars, sun, moon, and "winds of well-known names even though their directions might differ."[59]

It is a common requirement of literary, religious, and scientific meteorology that for a cloud to be available for analysis it must be represented in *logos*. The right use of names is widely acknowledged to be a precondition for theoretical inquiry, as here by the philosopher al-Fārābī (d. 339/950):

> It is not possible to verify the truth of an opinion we happen to hold by means of any old concept we happen to have, any more than we can be indifferent to arithmetic quantity, or the condition, composition, and order in which intelligible concepts present to us. Rather, for every opinion we seek to verify, we need well-defined concepts, known quantities, and ascertainment of the condition, composition, and order of things. This requires that the words expressing these be in the same condition as the words we submit to one another for verification. We therefore need rules that govern our concepts as well as the verbal expressions we use for them, in order to protect ourselves from error.[60]

Though not a work of Greek-inspired meteorology, nor a philosophical work in any way, the *Book of Rain* is scientific writing of the purest realism, aimed at the betterment of our discursive grasp on the phenomenal world.[61] Concerning the book's purpose, Abū Zayd makes no statement, but the scholastic literature of later periods offers plenty of yarns dramatizing the value of linguistic erudition. In another anecdote presented by Ibn Durayd, the Prophet himself deduces that the life-giving rain *al-Ḥayā* is imminent, on the basis of questions put to his companions:

> Ismāʿīl b. Aḥmad b. Ḥafṣ, who is the grammarian known as Samʿān al-Naḥwī, informed us that Abū ʿUmar al-Ḍarīr was informed by ʿAbbād b. ʿAbbād b. Ḥabīb b. al-Muhallab that Mūsā [b. Muḥammad] b. Ibrāhīm al-Taymī related on the authority of his father that his grandfather said:

> The Prophet, God's blessings and peace be upon him, was seated among his companions one day when there came into view a cloud. They said to him: "Now this, O Prophet of God, is a cloud."

"How does its foundation look to you?" he asked. "Excellent," they said, "and powerfully established."

"How does its axial rotation look to you?" he asked. "Excellent," they said. "It is wheeling energetically."

"How do its crowns look to you?" he asked. "Excellent," they said. "They are upraised firmly."

"How does its lightning look to you?" he asked. "Is it a flicker, a flash, or a forking fan?" "To be sure," they said, "it is a forking fan."

"And the proportion of its darkness to its brightness?" he asked. "Excellent," they said. "Its darkness is profound."

"It is *al-Ḥayā* 'The Life-Giver,'" he said, God's blessings and peace be upon him. "O Prophet of God," they said, "we have never seen anyone more eloquent (*afṣaḥ*) than you."

"How could it be otherwise," he said, "when the Qur'ān was revealed by means of 'the clear Arabic tongue' (*Sūrat al-Shu'arā'* 26:195) that is my tongue?"[62]

In this apocryphal hadith, mastery of traditional vocabulary obviates the need to look outside.[63]

While the *Book of Rain*'s self-evident purpose is to promote eloquence, anything to be said for this virtue remains external to the text, and a vindication of philological learning can join the long list of things that Abū Zayd's book is not. A lexicon is what it is, and what it establishes is a standard for the use of names. If this is the extent of the *Book of Rain*'s bequest to seekers after scientific knowledge, it is a substantial contribution.

♦

The *Book of Rain*'s greatest contribution to eco-consciousness might be in the *Book of Waters* (*Kitāb al-Miyāh*) conjoined to it under the subtitle "Names of Waters" (*Asmā' al-miyāh*). Al-Aṣma'ī had a *K. Miyāt al-'arab* (Book of the Waters of the Arabs), which was a work of geography detailing individual springs and wadis of the Arabian Peninsula.[64] By contrast, Abū Zayd's *K. al-Miyāh* has just one place-name in it: *Washḥā'*, and in order to discover that this was a water-source in the Najd belonging to the Banū Kilāb, one must look elsewhere.[65]

Abū Zayd's text is no geography but a typology of terrestrial waters and their interface with human need. Scarcity is a constant in this section of the *Book of Rain*, alternating (in the ABAB pattern described above) with words for abundance and activating their emotional charge. It was Mikhail Bakhtin's contention that in an alphabetically-ordered dictionary, this does not happen—that no matter how affecting a word's referent (Bakhtin's example is *radost'*, Russian for "joy"), it is emotive only *in potentia* until used in an utterance and made into a lived event.[66] In the *Book of Waters*, nothing is neutral, least of all the poetic citations where community access to water is a matter of honor and shame. Those who get their water from Washḥā', a poet says, can count on its renewal, and this is a point of Kilābī pride. Conversely, the community said to drink caustic brine (*ujāj*) unfit for wolves is being mocked for this reason. Context is crucial, because the desert traveler's ability to subsist on bad water was a boastworthy trait.[67] But collective access to salubrious drinking water was a point of tribal honor, as in the *Mu'allaqa* of 'Amr b. Kulthūm (fl. late sixth century CE):

> Where we show up to drink, the water's pure.
> Others have to drink from a turbid trickle.[68]

A community's access to water is a synecdoche of the community's fortune, and this recalls my opening remarks about the rain. But if rain falls at heaven's whim, groundwater is reached through expertise and hard labor. This is emphasized throughout *K. al-Bi'r* (Book of the Well) of Ibn al-A'rābī (d. 231/846), who quotes Abū Zayd:

> ***Aṣlada*** and *akdā* mean "to reach a hard place" in one's digging. Abū Zayd recited the verse (meter: *kāmil*):

O ʿUthmān, my well is dry. It is **sunk**
in hard rock, and resists all efforts to get a trickle going.[69]

The *Book of Rain* has less to say about water extraction. We learn words for canals and trenches, but not the tools for digging them. There is precise language for subterranean aquifers and catchments, which are age-old staples of human survival in the Arabian Peninsula, and these are poignant for a couple of reasons. For one, they hint at meagerness and difficulty of access, and lives lived and lost along the narrowest of hydrological margins. For another, the peninsula's subterranean deposits of fossil water have in our day been mined beyond return.[70] Any statistics I could give for this would soon be outdated, and in an ordinary work of classical philology they would be out of place, but they would give quantitative weight to the ecological lessons of the *Book of Rain*.

Philology is a pluralistic venture, says Sheldon Pollock (2014), requiring consciousness of three temporal planes, or three dimensions as he calls them. First is the historical plane of the text's genesis, and third is the present moment—the "here and now" of the editor/translator's subjective experience of the text. In between these points is the *longue durée* of its reception by hearers and readers, and their critical and creative responses to it, which make up the text's "tradition." There is cause for skepticism where Pollock is sanguine about disaggregating dimensions one and two, because (as pointed out above by Gregor Schoeler) tradition is not just metatext. Many texts are profoundly shaped by tradition (like Abū Zayd's *K. al-Nawādir*, described above), and some are pure products of it (like the *dīwān* of Majnūn Laylā, discussed ahead). The *Book of Rain* is a case where tradition and origin really can be considered separately, because the scholars who preserved it were so good about keeping their commentary external to the text. But for all the *Book of Waters* has to teach us, we can thank tradition in the persons of Abū ʿAbd Allāh al-Yazīdī or his uncle Abū Jaʿfar, one of whom decided it belonged in the *Book of Rain*.

Of the many landmarks of Arabic philology that might be translated here and now, no one will wonder why the *Book of Rain* was chosen. It is impossible to read a premodern book of rain and clouds and groundwater without thinking of modern climate and the alterations into which capitalism and combustion technology have sped it. Climate change is nothing new—the Negev became a desert less than 1,500 years ago—and neither is catastrophe. What is new are the scale and speed of quantitative changes that amount to qualitative, existential ones, and the anthropogenic causes driving them. The effect on rainfall in the Arabian Peninsula is counterintuitive, with a 20–40 percent *increase* in annual precipitation projected by the end of the twenty-first century—no general blessing but a patchwork of spatial and interannual disequilibria punctuated by extreme weather events.[71] To call this a "microcosm" of climate change globally is a little weird, given the peninsula's vast area, but it may yet be emblematic, leading me to one more way the *Book of Rain* can help absorb its lessons.

I refer to the poetic convention of *waṣf al-maṭar*—the motif rebranded by Ali Hussein (2009) as "lightning-scene," where poets describe a night they were kept awake by a storm, and the effects it has on all the territories it touches. (The one by Imru' al-Qays at the beginning of this introduction is the best-known example by far.) Abū Zayd presents the start of one lightning-scene by way of glossing *al-sudd*, the cloud so named for its "obstruction" of the sky (meter: *wāfir*):

> "Look! Do you see the blades of lightning
> sparking up and making straight for al-Afʿāh?"
> With my retinue of men, I sat to watch the clouds
> as they multiplied and **blocked the sky**, betokening rain.

There is much to say about this motif, and it is reserved for the notes ahead. Here I mean it to show what a localized event rainfall can be. In Europe and North America, the ordinary assumption is that when rain falls in one place, it's also raining a mile away.[72] Not so in the Arabian Peninsula, where rain can drench one valley and leave the plain beside it dry. This is borne out in Arabic poetry, where the lightning-scene unfolds at a distance, and the trials and blessings of the storm are for others to receive. Never have I seen one where the poet gets wet. This particular convention, where the one who witnesses and describes the rain gets no benefit from it, might in all seriousness be taken as an occasion to reflect on disparities of drought and precipitation globally, their increasing juxtaposition locally, and the inequalities of life and water security that go with this. If it sounds like I am proposing allegorical readings of the *Book of Rain* that Abū Zayd did not have in mind, that is absolutely right.

♦

The unique manuscript of the *Book of Rain* was published twice in quick succession by R. J. H. Gottheil (1896) and Louis Cheikho (1905), and has not been reedited since.[73] Dated to the year 631/1233-4, the manuscript is of such clarity that a facsimile edition would be as welcome as a new critical one. Gottheil's and Cheikho's misreadings of the text are more than several, but neither edition is terribly flawed. My corrections will be evident to anyone who reads either edition alongside this translation. Most are minor enough to pass over in silence, and where they are not minor there is a note.

In the translation, there are two decisions I should justify—one subtractive, the other additive, and neither one what Abū Zayd had in mind. In the subtractive column is the text's formal multiplicity. Along with nouns and names and epithets, the *Book of Rain*'s weather-words include many verb forms. To bring the text within range of English-language readability, it was necessary to curtail them, and so most verbs and participles have been suppressed. As an example of what's gone missing, I present the first few "Names of Rain" (corresponding to page 6 in the text ahead) with all omitted forms restored:

> The first of the names for rain is *al-qiṭqiṭ*. This is the finest of the rains, and slightly greater than *al-qiṭqiṭ* is *al-ra<u>dh</u>dhā<u>dh</u>*. *Qaṭqaṭat al-samāʾ* "The sky rained down in

> tiny grains," and [active participle] *muqaṭqiṭa* are both said, as is *aradhdhat* "It sprinkled," [with active participle] *muridhdha* and [verbal noun] *irdhādh*. The next rain greater is *al-ṭashsh*: *tashshat al-samāʾ* "The sky drizzled" and *taṭishshu* "It is drizzling" are said with [verbal noun] *ṭashsh*. Up from *al-ṭashsh* is *al-baghsha*: *baghashat* "It showered weakly" and *tabghashu* "It is showering weakly" are said with [verbal noun] *baghsh*. Up from that is *al-ghabya*, and *al-ḥalba* and *al-shajdha* are like it. *Aghbat* "It showered," [with active participle] *mughbiya*, and [verbal noun] *ighbāʾ* are said, and [so are] *ḥalabat* "It gave milk," *taḥlabat* "It is giving milk," [with verbal noun] *ḥalb*; and *ashjadhat* "It rained easingly," *sc.* "The rain eased," *tushjidhu* "It rains easingly," *sc.* "The rain is easing," [with verbal noun] *ishjādh*.

Faithful as this may be, it is repellent to eye and ear. In translation like this, the *Book of Rain* would not win a single reader.

In the additive column are the English-language labels I have devised for each lexeme in the *Book of Rain*—a poetic necessity without which the translation would have no life. Although these labels harmonize with Abū Zayd's text, they do not correspond to anything in it. Rarely in fact does the *Book of Rain* explain the lexical meaning of a word. For this, my main source is the dictionary of Ibn Manẓūr (d. 711/1312) called *Lisān al-ʿarab* (The Tongue of the Arabs), abbreviated throughout as *Lisān*. In nearly every case, it is my arbiter, as in the exemplary case of *naḍad*. Abū Zayd says that *al-naḍad* is a cloud similar to *al-ṣabīr* and *al-rukām*, that its plural is *al-anḍād*, and nothing more. To arrive at an English-language equivalent, I turn to *Lisān*'s entry for the root √*nḍd* and find the verb *naḍada* used in the first place for the act of making a heap of one's belongings. And then:

> *Al-naḍad* is a composite cloud. Ibn al-Aʿrābī recited the verse (meter: *ṭawīl*):
>
> The ruins at the barren, doe-colored tracts—why don't you interrogate them?
> My Lord has watered them with a rearing cloud accompanied by a ***naḍad***.[74]

As an epithet for the cloud, *al-naḍad* is an intuitive metaphor. The cloud's likeness to a heap of movable goods is easy to understand. (For what but its "heaped-up" appearance is a *cumulus* cloud so called?) My choice of an English-language label is clear, and even though Abū Zayd supplies no gloss, adding "The Heaped-Up" to his text does no violence.

Three more notes on method. (1) Convinced of the merits of giving English translations for Arabic book titles, I have adopted those already in use by other scholars (especially Ramzi Baalbaki and Gregor Schoeler) as much as possible, without pausing to give credit. (2) My endnotes include a great deal of translated material that is external to the *Book of Rain*—selections from classical poetry and prose demonstrating the uses of a given word (just as Ibn Manẓūr does in the above-quoted passage from *Lisān* art. √*nḍd*). Western scholarship calls this kind of thing by Latin names: *loci probantes* "evidentiary occurrences," *loci classici* "classical occurrences," and *testimonia*. The last of these is a close equivalent to *s̲h̲awāhid* (sg. *s̲h̲āhid*), which is the Arabic word for verses that "bear witness" to a given feature of the language. Their paucity in the *Book of Rain* was noted above: only twenty-six poetic verses are quoted in the text. My resolution to refrain from adding any did not last long. There is too much relevant material that is unknown in English, and it is too good to resist. Limiting myself to poets before Abū Zayd's day was no constraint at all. Readers who wish to experience the *Book of Rain* without this supplementary material can disregard the endnotes. Finally, (3) I have not felt any inclination to "tweak" the text artfully by smuggling in a made-up word (a vicious practice called in Arabic *tadlīs*). Had I succumbed to such an urge, I would not have omitted *"The Puffy."

My work on the *Book of Rain* began in 2010 during a residence in Cairo. In February 2011, I was able to consult microfilm of BnF MS 4231 Arabe (Ancien fonds arabe 1328) in Paris. For both opportunities I thank the Binational Fulbright Commission in Egypt.

♦

To be overrapt in the doings of heavenly bodies is a classic philosopher's foible, but in view of the heavens' grand regularity it is defensible. Stars and planets follow paths that are calculable, predictable, and available for steady contemplation. Clouds, by comparison, are ludicrously temporal. When we complain of time and fortune, saying they are fleeting, evanescent and fickle, we say so by analogy to the cloud. What is more, clouds move in time's direction only. By Laplace it was shown that Newton's planetary orbits run backward and forward with equal plausibility, but backwards-running footage of clouds fools no one. The main joke of Aristophanes's *Clouds*, as I understand it, is that only a loon would mistake them for objects of scientific knowledge. From geometric solids they are the furthest thing possible, and pathetically uninstructive compared to the clear night sky.

Does the joke still go over? I (who adore the *Clouds*) don't think so. People in our day seem better equipped to learn from nebulous entities. Who doubts there is wisdom in what comes to be and passes away? Or that the superlunary realm is bound by the same physical laws we live by on the earth? It was Michel Serres who taught me about Fourier, Carnot and the second law of thermodynamics, and the awareness of time's irreversibility that modern combustion science enforced.[75] Clouds are likewise machines that work in one temporal direction only, attended by lightning's combustive power. And like the river of Heraclitus, the same cloud is never gazed on twice.

At Amarna it was taught that the sun produced not only light, but time itself: the former through its rays, and the latter through its motion.[76] The clouds that shade the sun work that way too. Contemplating them, we experience time's passage, but what clouds are supposed to bring with time is rain.

NOTES

[1] First debunked in a paper presented by Laura Martin to the American Anthropological Association in 1982, and published in 1986 as "'Eskimo Words for Snow': A Case Study in the Genesis and Decay of an Anthropological Example." See more recently Cichocki and Kilarski (2010) and Krupnik and Müller-Wille (2010).

[2] Noted by al-Jāḥiẓ (d. 255/869) in *K. al-Bayān wa-l-tabyīn* (The Book of Lucidity and Elucidation), I.20: "In the Qur'ān, you will find *al-maṭar* mentioned only in the spirit of retribution. And yet most speakers of Arabic, elite and commonfolk alike, observe no distinction between *maṭar* and *ghayth*."

[3] Last twelve verses of the 78-verse *Muʿallaqa* (meter: *ṭawīl*). al-Zawzani, *Sharḥ al-Muʿallaqāt al-sabʿ*, 37–41. All translations by David Larsen, unless otherwise credited.

[4] Verses 5–8 of a 31-verse poem (meter: *kāmil*), no. 8 in *al-Mufaḍḍaliyyāt* (Poems Collected by al-Mufaḍḍal al-Ḍabbī), 44–45, cited in Abū Suwaylim (1987), 140–41.

[5] Schoeler (2006), 39. For a lexicography-specific example, see Hämeen-Anttila (2004), 141–48.

[6] Schoeler (2006), 33, notes that the same might be asked of the *Course of General Linguistics*, which would have no existence as a text without the lecture notes and editorial efforts of Ferdinand de Saussure's students.

[7] Baalbaki (2014), 16–23.

[8] Quoted by Jalāl al-Dīn al-Suyūṭī (d. 911/1505) from the lost *Amālī* (Dictations) of Thaʿlab (d. 291/904); in *al-Muzhir fī ʿulūm al-lugha* (Bringer of Light to the Language Sciences) I.151 and *al-Iqtirāḥ fī ʿilm uṣūl al-naḥw* (An Extemporaneous Study of the Principles of Grammar), 207. Where al-Jāḥiẓ names "the highlanders of Tamīm, the lowlanders of Qays and the rump of Hawāzin" as bywords for linguistic purity (*K. al-Bayān wa-l-tabyīn* I.70), he is paraphrasing his teacher Abū Zayd.

[9] *Muzhir* I.207. At *Muzhir* II.483, al-Suyūṭī quotes misleading commentary from *al-ʿUmda* (The Pillar) I.134 of Ibn Rashīq al-Qayrawānī (d. 456/1063 or 463/1070) that identifies these highlands with the area around Medina. Federico Corriente (1976), 67, considered it forged.

[10] Ibn Jinnī, *al-Khaṣāʾiṣ* II.12; Schub (1974).

[11] The verb *yaʾisa* means "to despair," but for the Hawāzin it was a verb of knowing, and thus it is heard in *Sūrat al-Raʿd*: "Do those who believe not **know** (*a-fa-lam **yayʾasi***) that God would have led all of humanity [to Him], had He so willed?" Rājiḥī (1969), 200.

[12] Carter (1990), 106–7.

[13] Lecker (1997).

14 ʿAlī b. Yūsuf al-Qifṭī (d. 646/1248), *Inbāh al-ruwāt* (The Narrators' Roll Call) II.34; see Sayyid (1980), 17 and 35.

15 "Caliphal tastes were overwhelmingly for expertise in nighttime chatter, carousal, and the art of storytelling … areas in which Abū Zayd, with his focus on rarities and peculiarities of language, did not excel." Aḥmad (1980), 26. Ibn al-Nadīm (*Fihrist*, I.154), however, reports that Abū Zayd was invited to Baghdad during the caliphate of al-Mahdī (r. 158–169/775–785).

16 The *Mughnī* (Summa) of al-Qāḍī ʿAbd al-Jabbār (d. 415/1025) lists Abū Zayd among the grammarians who professed Muʿtazilite doctrine (VII.218), noted by van Ess (1992), II.476.

17 *Marātib al-naḥwiyyīn*, 43.

18 Al-Khaṭīb al-Baghdādī (d. 463/1071), *Tārīkh Baghdād* (History of Baghdad) IX.80,, al-Qifṭī, *Inbāh al-ruwāt* II.32.

19 Rosenthal (1956), 10n5; Szombathy (2004).

20 The roster of Sībawayh's teachers is a matter of debate; for Abū Zayd, see Versteegh (1993), 163.

21 Bauer (1994), 113–15.

22 Ibn Khālawayh's transmission statement (*Qaraʾtu kutub Abī Zayd ʿalā Abī ʿUmar ʿan Thaʿlab ʿan Ibn Najda ʿan Abī Zayd*) was taken by Brockelmann (*GAL* I.125) for a statement of authorship—a misunderstanding carried into Nagelborg's 1909 edition of *K. al-Shajar*, which was published as Ibn Khālawayh's work.

23 Abū l-Ṭayyib describes Ibn Najda as a student of Abū Zayd's who specialized in recitations of his master's teachings (*Marātib al-naḥwiyyīn*, 94).

24 Wild (1987), 137; Baalbaki (2014), 36–45 and 87–89.

25 *K. al-Nawādir*, ed. Aḥmad (1981), 567, 609.

26 Sellheim (2002).

27 In *al-Fihrist*, I.154, and elsewhere the title appears as إيمان عثمان : *Īmān ʿUthmān* (The Belief of ʿUthmān). It was emended to أيمان عيمان : *Aymān ʿaymān* by Khalīl al-ʿAṭiyya (1990), 22, on the strength of *Lisān* art. √ʿ*ym*, where the inverted phrase *ʿaymān aymān* is attested as an expression for calamitous poverty: "A man whose camels have left him and whose wife has died is said to be *ʿaymān aymān*." Someone else who got it right was Aḥmad Fāris al-Shidyāq (1804–1887) in *al-Jāsūs ʿalā l-Qāmūs* (The Snooper into al-Fīrūzābādī's Great Dictionary), 128, probably thanks to Ibn Khālawayh's *K. Laysa fī kalām al-ʿarab* (The Book of "Not in the Arabic Language"), 123–24. Abū Zayd's book was perhaps a collection of rhyming proverbs.

28 Where cited by Ibn Jinnī in *al-Khaṣāʾiṣ* I.97, and al-Lablī (d. 691/1292) in *Tuḥfat al-majd*, 298, it's apparent that *K. Ḥīla wa-maḥāla* is a work of morphology, probably similar to *K. Faʿaltu wa-afʿaltu* listed ahead.

29 In some editions of the *Fihrist*, the title appears as *al-Hawsh wa-l-nawsh* (Armed and Unarmed Combat).

30 "Goats" (المعزى) is read in some editions of the *Fihrist* as *al-Muʿaddā* (المعدى) "The Transitive," and elsewhere as *al-Mafdī* (المفدى) "The Ransomed." But Abū Zayd's book on goats is confirmed in *Muʿjam al-udabāʾ* (Dictionary of the Scholars) III.1362 by Yāqūt (d. 626/1229), who credits him not only with *K. al-Miʿzā* but a *Naʿt al-ghanam* (Qualities of Goat-kind), an apparent duplicate. *Lisān* art. √*jhā* attributes a *K. al-Ghanam* (Book of Goatkind) to Abū Zayd, which might be a slip for the *K. al-Ghanam* of Abū ʿUbayd mentioned in *Lisān* art. √*ḥdʾ*.

31 Variantly read as *al-Qarāʾin* (End Rhymes).

32 The reading of the Qurʾān with canonical status at Basra was that of Abū ʿAmr b. al-ʿAlāʾ (d. 154/770), another of Abū Zayd's teachers. Abū Zayd's attention to variant readings of the Qurʾān is appreciable in the *Book of Rain*, where the only Qurʾānic reference is to a variant of *Sūrat al-Raʿd* 13:17 (page 18).

33 A version of this text survives in the margins of the unique MS of *K. al-Hamz* (described above) where it was inscribed by a later hand. Louis Cheikho, the editor of *K. al-Hamz*, called it a foul copy (*K. al-Hamz*, 3).

34 Al-Murtaḍā al-Zabīdī (d. 1205/1790) says in *Tāj al-ʿarūs* (The Bridegroom's Crown) I.206, art. √*k̲h̲bʾ* that Abū Zayd entitled one of his books *K. al-Khubʾa* (or *al-Khabʾa*) because it began with the proverb: *Khubʾatun khayrun min yafaʿati sawʾin* "A daughter who stays home is better than a grown son who is no good." If this was a book of proverbs, perhaps it was identical to the *K. al-Amthāl* listed ahead.

35 Variantly read as *al-Ḥilsa* (The Saddlecloth).

36 A digest of this text survives as a single unbound leaf found tucked into an unrelated codex in Istanbul's Ragıp Paşa Library (MS 1476). On this sheet are twenty-seven proverbial expressions with short commentaries, as selected from Abū Zayd's *K. al-Amthāl* (Book of Proverbial Expressions) by ʿAlī b. Muḥammad al-Nīlī. (early eighth/fourteenth century) and recopied by the famous litterateur ʿAbd al-Qādir b. ʿUmar al-Baghdādī (d. 1093/1682). The sheet of paper's 1985 discovery by Jalīl al-ʿAṭiyya was followed by publication in the journal *al-Mawrid* for 1986.

37 Perhaps identical to the above-mentioned *K. al-Lughāt.*

38 Baalbaki (2014), 161, 267.

39 al-Lughawī, *Marātib al-naḥwiyyīn*, 42–43.

40 Foucault (1994), 132.

41 Daston (2012), 167–74.

42 Popper (1951), De Putter et al. (1998).

43 Le Roy Ladurie (1988), Chuine et al. (2004).

44 The surmise of Baalbaki (2014), 136–37, that the *Book of Trees* and *Book of Herbage* were two separate works conjoined later (after the fashion of the *Book of Rain* and *Book of Waters*) doesn't weaken Bauer's point. Whether books or chapters, the lack of overlap between the two (no plant is treated as tree *and* herb) shows classificatory principle at work.

45 Bauer (1994), 115.

46 Lloyd (1964). Eastern prototypes for the doctrine (attributed to Anaximander, d. ca. 546 BCE) are always possible, if hard to pin down. Conger (1952), 115; Nie (2016).

47 *Mukhtār rasāʾil Jābir b. Ḥayyān* (Selected Epistles of Jābir) I.21–22.

48 The shortcomings of this text were noted by al-Jāḥiẓ in *K. al-Ḥayawān* (The Book of Animals) VI.280. It is now recognized as a translation of some Hellenistic-era redaction of Aristotle's text, as identified in Endress (1974), also Endress (1992) and Lettink (1999), 7.

49 Sersen (1976), 144–45. Ibn al-Khammār's translation was edited and translated into English by Daiber (1992), 166–293.

50 *Contra* Sersen, Daiber (1992), 222n75, contends that al-Kindī's primary meteorological source text was indeed Aristotle's, "perhaps with a Hellenistic commentary which might have adapted some non-Aristotelian and ultimately Theophrastean ideas."

51 *Rasāʾil al-Kindī al-falsafiyya* (Philosophical Epistles of al-Kindī) II.71.

52 The point of the marginal note may seem contradictory, so let me press it twice. The report that Abū Zayd related this hadith may be 100 percent authentic, and could well reflect his sincere belief. But the fact that it was jotted in the margin by a latter-day copyist (to all appearances, the same seventh-/thirteenth-century hand that was responsible for the rest of the manuscript) means that Abū Zayd did not put it in the *Book of Rain* himself.

53 Varisco (1987) and Varisco (1991).

54 "This term originally, and most properly, was used for a calendar inscribed on stone exhibited in a public space in a Greek city. The inscription gave a list of the rising and setting times of the stars and the kind of weather associated with them. Since the astronomical year did not keep in step with the civil year, the dates of the civil calendar were indicated on pegs inserted into holes adjacent to the lines of text; hence the term *parapēgma*, from the verb meaning 'to fix beside.' The system enabled the calendar to be used over a long period of time. Alongside of, or deriving from, this epigraphic form, there developed a literary form of the *parapēgma*, in which a fixed set of dates for the rising and setting of the significant stars was given. This form is represented by Columella's *De re rustica*, book XI, Ptolemy's *Phaseis*, and works attributed to Quintilian and Aëtios of Amida." Bos and Burnett, introduction to al-Kindī (2000), 5–6.

55 *K. al-Ḥayawān* III.140. For comparison, consider the *libri fulgorales* of Etruscan discipline described in Turfa (2012), and their Babylonian prototypes in Gehlken (2012).

56 Ibn Qutayba, *K. al-Anwāʾ*, 175. Verse 10 of a 23-verse poem in *Dīwān al-Nābigha*, 63 (meter: *basīṭ*).

57 Ibn Durayd, *K. Waṣf al-maṭar*, 6–7; cf. Ibn Qutayba, *K. al-Anwāʾ*, 177, and Ibn Abī l-Dunyā, *K. al-Maṭar*, 63.

58 Perceptively does Hämeen-Anttila (2002), 66–73, identify *waṣf al-maṭar* with the epic convention of *teikhoskopia*, in which one character explicates battlefield matters to another (as Helen to Priam in book III of the *Iliad*, or Sanjaya to Dhritarashtra throughout *Bhagavad Gita*).

59 *The Epistle on Legal Theory*, tr. Lowry, 17.

60 Al-Fārābī, *Iḥṣāʾ al-ʿulūm* (Catalogue of the Sciences), 34.

61 Arnaldez and Massignon (1963), 394.

62 Ibn Durayd, *K. Waṣf al-maṭar*, 3–5. The hadith appears in the *K. al-Nawādir* of Ibn al-Aʿrābī, 35–37, and was subsequently much repeated.

63 The hadith is negated (*munkar*) by the presence of Mūsā al-Taymī in its chain of transmission, Mūsā being reckoned an unreliable source by hadith scholars: thus Abū Jaʿfar al-ʿUqaylī (d. 322/934) in *Kitāb al-Ḍuʿafāʾ al-Kabīr* (The Big Book of Weak Narrators) IV.169.

64 *Al-Fihrist* I.157; Shakʿa (1991), 140. In one place (*Tāj al-ʿarūs* III.43, art. √*sḥb*), al-Zabīdī mentions a book by al-Aṣmaʿī on the names of clouds, but prior to this eighteenth-century statement no other mention of it can be found.

65 Yāqūt, *Muʿjam al-buldān* (The Dictionary of Countries) V.377, where Abū Zayd is cited to the effect that "*wash̲ḥāʾ* is an epithet for a goat with white markings that resemble a variegated sash." Whether Washḥāʾ was so called after its goats, or through some other connection to the sash called *al-wis̲hāḥ*, is anyone's guess.

66 Bakhtin (1986), 87; Larsen (2015), 130; cf. Tynianov (1980), 64–73.

67 Papoutsakis (2009), 79–82. Dhū l-Rumma's verses in note lxxvi to *al-kawkab* exemplify this.

68 Al-Zawzanī, *Sharḥ al-Muʿallaqāt al-sabʿ*, 134 (verse 77 of a 94-verse poem, meter: *wāfir*).

69 *K. al-Biʾr*, 56.

70 Odhiambo (2017), Varisco (2017).

71 Rao et al. (2024).

72 Cusk (1997), 7.

73 The 1908 reprint of Cheikho's edition was the basis for Jumʿa (1993), a study that includes an alphabetical reordering of the *Book of Rain*'s contents.

74 The verse is first of an eleven-line poem by Ibn al-Dumayna (mid-second/eighth century), appearing with variations in *Dīwān Ibn al-Dumayna*, 56.

75 Serres (1982), 71–72.

76 Assmann (2010), 37–38.

بسم الله الرحمن الرحيم الاعتماد على رب العباد

قال أبو زيد الانصاري قال القيسيون أول المطر
الوسمي وانواؤه العرقوتان المؤخرتان من الدلو
ثم الشرط ثم الثريا وبين كل نجمين نحو من خمس عشرة
ليلة ثم الشتوي بعد الوسمي وانواؤه الجوزاء ثم
الذراعان ونثرتهما ثم الجبهة وهي آخر الشتوي
واول الدفي وانواؤه آخر الجبهة والعواء ثم
الصرفة وهي فصل بين الدفي والصيف ثم
الصيف وانواؤه السماكان الاول والأعزل
والاخر الرقيب وما بين السماكين صيف وهو نحو
من اربعين ليلة ثم الحميم وهو نحو من عشرين
ليلة الى خمس عشرة عند طلوع الدبران وهو
بين الصيف والخريف وليس له نوء ثم الخريف
وانواؤه النسران ثم الاخضر ثم عرقوتا
الدلو الأوليان وكل مطر من الوسمي الى الدفي

الوسمي العرقوتان
الثريا
الشتوي الجوزاء
الذراعان الجبهة
الدفي العواء
الصرفة الصيف
السماكان الأعزل
الرقيب
الحميم
الدبران
الخريف نوء
النسران الأخضر
عرقوتا الدلو

THE BOOK OF RAIN

BY ABŪ ZAYD SAʿĪD B. AWS AL-ANṢĀRĪ
(d. ca. 215/830)

as set down by Abū ʿAbd Allāh Muḥammad b. al-ʿAbbās b. Muḥammad b. Abī Muḥammad Yaḥyā b. al-Mubārak al-Yazīdī (d. 310/922),

from his uncle Abū Jaʿfar Aḥmad b. Muḥammad al-Yazīdī (d. shortly before 260/873-4),

from Abū Zayd, may God have mercy on him.

In the name of God, the Merciful, the Compassionate.
Worshippers of the Lord may rely on Him.

Abū Zayd al-Anṣārī said:

[ASTERISMS AND SEASONS]

The tribesmen of Qays[i] say: First of the rains is *al-wasmī* "The Mark-Maker."○ Its asterisms○ are *al-ʿArquwatān al-Muʾakhkharatān min al-Dalw* "The Latter Bucket-Timbers" [αβ Pegasi], then *al-Sharaṭ* "The Fore-Runner" [βγ Arietis] and then *al-Thurayyā* "The Pleiades." These constellations are separated from each other by intervals of some fifteen nights.

After *al-wasmī* comes *al-shatwī* "Winter Rain." Its asterisms are *al-Jawzāʾ*○

○ *AL-WASMĪ* gets its name from *wasm*, which is a "brand" for marking livestock. This name is for the rain that marks bare ground with vegetative growth.

○ ASTERISMS: For the workings of *al-anwāʾ*, see the Introduction, page xxvi, and Miller (2024), 171. For the sake of clarity, Abū Zayd's account of the *wasmī* asterisms may be restated like this:

There is a fifteen-day period during which the pair of stars known as the Latter Bucket-Timbers are visible just above the eastern horizon at daybreak. This period corresponds roughly to late September, which is when Central Arabia's dry season ends. Fifteen days later, the Latter Bucket-Timbers are replaced in the dawn sky by another pair of stars, and fifteen days after that the Pleiades take over. Throughout this forty-five-day period, any rain that falls is called a *wasmī* rain.

○ *AL-JAWZĀʾ* has long been identified with the Ptolemaic sign of Gemini, but before that it was the name of a traditional Arabian superconstellation of much greater size, spanning the middle (*jawz*) of the sky, and overlapping Orion.[ii] *Al-Jawzāʾ* was a female figure, and various stars and star-groups were named after her armor, throne, footstool, and various body parts.[iii] The star that is her foot (*rijl*) is called in English *Rigel*. The asterism referred to here is more precisely *Raʾs al-Jawzāʾ*, the figure's head.

[$\lambda\varphi^1\varphi^2$ Orionis], and then *al-Dhiraʿān* "The Two Arms"○ [αβ Geminorum] and *al-Nathra* "The Septum" [εγδ Cancri], followed by *al-Jabha* "The Forehead" [ζγημα Leonis] which presides over the last of the *shatwī* rains and the first of the *dafīʾ*.

Al-dafīʾ "Heating Rain" begins in the latter part of *al-Jabha*. It lasts through the asterisms of *al-ʿAwwāʾ* "The Howler"○ [βηγδε Virginis] and then *al-Ṣarfa* "The Change"○ [β Leonis], which divides *al-dafīʾ* from *al-ṣayyif*.

The asterisms of *al-ṣayyif* "Summertime Rain" are two. The first is *al-Simāk al-Aʿzal* "The Unarmed *Simāk*"○ [Spica Virginis], and the latter is *al-Simāk al-Raqīb* "The Watchful *Simāk*" [Arcturus]. *Al-ṣayyif* is the rain that falls between them, a period that lasts about forty nights.

○ THE TWO ARMS, the septum, and the forehead mentioned here belong to another Arabian superconstellation called *al-Asad* "The Lion," which antedates the Ptolemaic sign of Leo.[iv]

○ *AL-ʿAWWĀʾ* is variously identified; here it refers to δ Virginis, or to βηγδε Virginis as a group. "The Howler" either signifies a dog, or a pack of them—or the name is connected to another sense of *ʿawā*, "to curve," which would make *al-ʿAwwāʾ* "The Bent Figure."[v]

○ *AL-ṢARFA* is an equinoctial sign. At one time of year, it indicates a change to warmer temperatures; at another, it indicates the opposite.[vi]

○ *AL-SIMĀK* is usually glossed as something like "The Lofty" but its derivation isn't clear. The Unarmed *Simāk* is so called because "unlike its counterpart, it holds no weapon," according to *Adab al-kātib* (The State Secretary's Handbook) of Ibn Qutayba; and the Watchful *Simāk* is so called for "the star in front of it, which they call its 'lance.'"[vii] For this reason, the Watchful *Simāk* is also called *al-Simāk al-Rāmiḥ* (the "Lance-Bearing *Simāk*"). In the early twentieth century, Alois Musil reported that the Rwala Bedouin of North Arabia called the season between winter and summer by the name *al-Smāk*.[viii]

Al-ḥamīm "The Hottest Part of the Year" follows it and lasts between fifteen and twenty nights during the auroral rising of *al-Dabarān* "The Follower"○ [α Tauri]. It comes between *al-ṣayyif* and *al-kharīf* but has no asterism.

Next is *al-kharīf* "Autumn."○ Its asterisms are *al-Nasrān* "The Two Eagles" [βγα Aquilae, α Lyrae], followed by *al-Akhḍar* "The Blue"○ [ε Pegasi?] and then *ʿArquwatā l-Dalw al-Awwaliyān* "The Prior Bucket-Timbers" [δγ Pegasi].

Any rain that falls from the *wasmī* period to the *dafīʾ* is called *rabīʿ* "Spring Rain."

The asterisms are in effect even when their stars cannot be seen.

Al-qayẓ "High summer"○ begins with the rising of the Pleiades, and ends with the rising of Canopus. *Al-ṣafariyya* "The season of increase" begins with the rising of Canopus, and ends with the rising of *al-Simāk*. The first forty nights of *al-ṣafariyya* alternate between moderate[ix] cool and warmth. *Al-shitāʾ* "Winter" begins with *al-Simāk*, and ends with the setting of *al-Jabha*. *Al-dafīʾ* "The Heating"

○ *AL-DABARĀN* is either Aldebaran (α Tauri) or the little constellation around it called the Hyades (αγδεθ Tauri). According to *Lisān* art. √*dbr*, it gets its name because it "follows" (*yadburu*) the Pleiades.

○ *AL-KHARĪF* is cognate with Hebrew *ḥoref* "winter," but connects more immediately with Arabic *kharafa* "to harvest dates," making it an odd fit within a pastoral-nomadic calendar, and seemingly a late adoption in the Najd.[x] Here it threatens to scuttle Abū Zayd's sequence, in which the *wasmī* rains were said to be the first to fall after the dry season.

○ THE BLUE for *al-Akhḍar* is archaic usage. *Akhḍar* now means "green," but early on it was used for blue and green (and sometimes black), and thus the sky was called *al-khaḍrāʾ*, and the sea *khuḍāra*.

○ *AL-QAYẒ* shares a Semitic root with Hebrew *qayitz*, meaning "fruit of summer," and by extension summer itself (as at Genesis 8:22).

begins with the setting of *al-Jabha*, and ends with *al-Ṣarfa*. *Al-ṣayf*[xi] "Summer" begins with *al-Simāk al-Aʿzal*, which is the first *Simāk*. It ends with the latter *Simāk* called "The Watchful." Between them are forty nights or so.

[NAMES OF RAIN]

First of the names for rain is *al-qiṭqiṭ* "The Tiny Grain." This is the finest of the rains. Slightly greater than *al-qiṭqiṭ* is the rain called *al-radhdhādh* "The Sprinkle," and the next rain greater is *al-ṭashsh* "The Drizzle." Up from *al-ṭashsh* is *al-baghsha* "The Weak Shower," and up from that is *al-ghabya* "The Shower."

Al-ḥalba "The Milking," *al-shajdha* "The Easing," *al-ḥafsha* "The Frisk,"○ and *al-ḥashka* "The Swelling" are showers of the same degree as *al-ghabya*.

Al-dīma is "continual" rain without thunder or lightning, lasting no less than a third of one day or night. Most rains do not last this long.

Al-tahtān "The Outpouring" is a kind of continual rain. A poet said (meter: *rajaz*):

Yā ḥabbadhā nadkhuki[xii] *bi-l-mashāfiri*
ka-annahu ***tahtānu*** *yawmin māṭiri*

I praise the discharge flying from your nostrils
like the **outpour** of a rainy day.

Two other continual rains are *al-haḍb* "Hard Rain" and *al-haṭl* "The Spatter." A poet said (meter: *ṭawīl*):

○ *AL-ḤAFSHA*: *Lisān* art. √*ḥfsh* defines this word as "a hard rain that stops after one hour." Its affiliated verb *ḥafasha*, said of a horse, means "to caper"; said of a woman, it means to awaken a man's lust by moving her body.[xiii]

Bi-Dhī r-Raḍmi min dhāti l-mazāhiri adjanat
ʿalayhā dhihābu ṣ-ṣayfi ***tahḍibuhā haḍban***

At Dhū l-Raḍm, the tended fires were overshadowed
by passing rains of summer that **came down hard**.

Al-dhihāb○ "Passing rains" can be either weak or strong.

Cloud cover that darkens the sky and brings no rain is called *al-dujunna*[xiv] "The Overcast." Its verb is *adjana* [heard in the above-quoted verse]. Days and nights so affected are described adjectivally as *dajn* and *dujunna*: "the day was *dajn*," "the day was *dujunna*," and in the genitive: "a day of *dajn*," "a day of *dujunna*." Active participle *dājina* describes a raincloud that covers the sky and delivers continual rain, and *dajn* is a word for plentiful rain.

Of all the *dīma* rains, the kind called *al-rihma* "The Discharge" falls the hardest and is the first to pass away. *Al-hafāʾa* "The Flap" is similar to *al-rihma*. Al-ʿAnbarī○ pronounced this word as *al-afāʾa*.

Yet another sort of *dīma* is the light rain called *al-daththa* "The Scotch Mist." Similar to it is the rain called *al-hadma* "The Nebuline." *Al-watfāʾ* "The Beetle-

○ *AL-DHIHĀB* is a plural noun, whose singular form (*dhihba*) is seldom encountered and does not occur in the *Book of Rain*. "Passing" is for its root in the verb *dhahaba*, meaning "to go" and "pass away," transience being an essential property of rain.

○ ʿANBARĪ designates a tribal subgroup of Tamīm called Banū l-ʿAnbar, who were thickly settled at Basra. Here it designates an individual ʿAnbarī, and by extension the group's dialect. A number of ʿAnbarīs served as judges at Basra, most eminently ʿUbayd Allāh b. al-Ḥasan b. Ḥuṣayn al-ʿAnbarī (d. 168/785).[xv] His name is nowhere mentioned in connection with Abū Zayd, but it's possible these two Basrans got together over poetry more than once. At the time of ʿUbayd Allāh's death Abū Zayd would have been about forty years old.

Brow"○ is a briskly-flowing rain that is counted among the continual rains, whether it is of long or short falling.

Al-qaṭr "Droplets" is said for all rain, weak and strong, as is *al-dhihāb*. A diffuse fall of light droplets is called *al-rashsh* "The Spray." The most abundant rain with the biggest droplets is called *al-wābil* "The Downpour." *Al-jawd* "Abundance" is said for profuse rain falling at any time of year. A poet said (meter: *rajaz*):

Anā l-jawādu bnu Jawādin bni Sabal
in dayyamū ***jāda*** *wa-in jādū wabal*

I am Jawād, son of Jawād○ ibn Sabal.
When others shed rain, **his rain is abundant**, and when others abound he's a downpour.

○ THE BEETLE-BROW is one of several names for rain and clouds deriving from words for hair—in this case *al-waṭaf*, which means "profuse hairiness of the eyebrows and eyelashes." Said of a rainstorm, it names the outer edges, and thus the geographic perimeter of a fall of rain.[xvi]

○ *JAWĀD* is a man's name, cognate with *al-jawd*, connoting generosity and abundance. In *Lisān* art. √*sbl* the poet is identified as Jahm b. Sabal, "a highly accomplished poet of the Banū Bakr." The initial pronoun changes from "I" to "he," and the boast is not about the poet's lineage but his horse's. *Sabal* was the name of a prize brood-mare of the pre-Islamic Arabs, and Jawād is additionally an epithet for a horse that puts on speed for long distances. In either case, man or horse, "giving profusely" is the property shared by *Jawād* and the rain called *al-jawd*.

Al-ʿAnbarī pronounced *dayyamū* in this verse as *dawwamū*.

When shares of a thing come in continuous succession, the whole is called *al-midrār*○ and *al-dirra* "The Torrent." This may be said of any rain. *Al-rikk* "The Lean" is a weak rain of no benefit unless it is followed by *al-tabiʿa* "The Consequent," which is one rain coming after another.

Al-sāḥiya "The Inundation" is an epithet of *al-wābil*, and vice versa: both *wābilun sāḥiyatun* "an inundating downpour" and *sāḥiyatun wābilun* "a downpouring inundation" are heard. It is said for the rain that scours everything it touches and sweeps it all away. When abundant rains grip the earth to the point that its depths are uprooted, its topsoil becomes its bottom, its hidden parts are made visible, and its visible parts are hidden, it is said to be *masḥūra* "ensorcelled." The rain called *jārr al-ḍabuʿ* "The Hyena Driver" never falls without setting the earth aflow, and is so called because it penetrates the hyena's den and sends it fleeing.[xvii]

Al-muḥtafal○ "The Aggregation" is a brisk, unflagging rain. Similar to it is *al-saḥḥ* "The Flow," with the difference that in *al-saḥḥ* individual droplets may not

○ *AL-MIDRĀR* is heard three times in the Qurʾān: twice as beneficial rain (*Sūrat al-Anʿām* 6:6, *Sūrat Hūd* 11:52), and in the tale of Noah as a torrent of destructive rain (*Sūrat Nūḥ* 71:11, quoted by Ibn Khālawayh in *On the names of the wind*, page 68).

○ *AL-MUḤTAFAL* has two possible meanings with respect to rain. One is the sense of "utmost output," in which (like *al-jawd*, above) *muḥtafil* is said of a horse when it runs at full strength (*Lisān* art. √*ḥfl*). This sense aligns with Abū Zayd's definition of *al-muḥtafal* as rain that is *ḥathīth*: "brisk," and more literally "spurred on."

The word has another sense, consistent with *iḥtafala*'s intransitive meanings "to gather together," "to collect" and "to fill up," said of wells and wadis when they fill up with water. Of rain it names the moment of its "coming together," that is, its perceived materialization from within the cloud.[xviii]

be visible. *Al-munhamir* "The Effluent" is like *al-saḥḥ*, as is *al-wadq*○ "The Influx." *Al-ḍarb* "The Stroke" is used for light rain, as is *al-qaṭr*, and *al-dihān* "The Gentle Strokes" are much the same. *Al-murwiya*[xix] "The Water-Bringers" are rains that irrigate the earth, while *al-mulabbid* "The Damper" wets its surface and causes the dust to settle. *Al-ḥayā* "The Life-Giver" is abundant rain. Successive bursts of rainfall are called *ahāḍīb*, which is the plural of *hiḍāb*, which is itself the plural of *haḍb* [the "Hard Rain" mentioned earlier]. *Al-halal* "The Incipient" is the beginning of rain. *Al-mut̲h̲ʿanjir* "The Plenisher" and *al-musḥanfir* "The Widespread" are plentiful in their flow.[xx]

Al-waliyy "The Close Companion" is said for rain that follows rain at any time.[xxi] *Al-ʿahd* "The Pledge" is a first rain. Land that is touched by a "shiver" of rain is said to be *muʿahhada* "impledged," and where rain has fallen evenly, the land is said to be *maʿhūda* "fulfilled." Rain that skips one area and falls on another is called *al-nufḍa* "a shiver." So too is *s̲h̲uʾbūb* "Cloudburst" said for rain that falls in one location without touching others; its plural is *s̲h̲aʾābīb*, and *al-najw* "The Wind Breaker," is similar to it. And land that is *manṣūḥa* "satisfied" has been blessed with abundant rain.

Al-g̲h̲ayt̲h̲ is a name for rain in general. *Al-sabal* "The Trailing Garment" is rain that hangs between cloud and earth, from the point of its leaving the cloud to its impact on the ground. A rain of little breadth may be called *al-saḥāba* "a

○ *AL-WADQ* names the "influx" or "incursion" of the contents of a cloud onto the terrestrial plane. Every cognate of this word signifies pressure at some corporeal boundary. *Al-wadaq* is the bulging of a paunch, *al-widāq* is a mare's desire to be mounted by the stallion, and invasive midday heat from which there is no escape is called *al-wadīqa*.

A pitched battle is called *d̲h̲āt* ***wadqayn*** "an occasion **of mutual incursion**," which might suggest *"The Bout" as an idiomatic equivalent to *al-wadq*. But a *bout* is an interval (of fighting, drinking, or what have you), and duration is not at issue with *al-wadq*.[xxii]

cloud," whether its drops are few or many, much like *al-shuʾbūb*. Similar to *al-sabal* are *al-ʿathānīn* "The Chin Hairs,"○ which is another name for rain [that dangles] between cloud and earth.

[FROST AND DEW]

Al-ḍarīb "The Striker," *al-ṣaqīʿ* "The Frost," and *al-jalīd* "Hard Frost" occur only under cloudless nighttime skies. *Al-thalj* "The Rime" can occur at night and on days of fog. A land whose plants are singed by frost is said to be *ḍariba* "stricken."[xxiii]

Terrestrial moisture○ left by rain or frost is called *al-ṭall* "The Dew." This word is also for the sap that the veins of a plant distribute to its branches. *Al-saqīṭ* "The Hoar" is another type of dew that emerges when the sky is *jardāʾ* or "bare of haze." The *taṣalluʿ* "balding" of the sky is the clearing of its haze. When it has cleared up completely, *al-ṣaḥw* "sobering up" is said to have occurred. The halting of the rain is called *al-iqṣār* "curtailment" and *al-iqlāʿ* "cessation."

[The verb *ṭalla* is used in different ways.] *Ṭulla l-qawm* "The people were dampened" is said when the dew affects them, leaving them *maṭlūlūn* "beset by damp."[xxiv] Blood that is *maṭlūl* has been "shed without penalty," when the identity of the killer is known but no action is taken.[xxv] [The verb *hadara* is similarly used:] ***Hadara*** *damuhu* "His blood **went for nought**" is said when the killer is

○ CHIN HAIRS are mentioned in the Appendix as attributes of the wind, specifically its front or foremost part, made visible by the debris it carries. If the *ʿathānīn* of the wind jut forward, it is natural for *ʿathānīn* of the rain to dangle down.

○ TERRESTRIAL MOISTURE translates *nadā*, a word for "moisture from an unseen source," and an ordinary expression for material largesse.[xxvi] It has more positive associations than *ṭall*, the word for "dew" that Abū Zayd uses *nadā* to define.

known and the powers that be take no action. [*Aṭlala*, a IVth-form verb, is heard in the expression "**I heaped** abuse upon him":] ***Aṭlaltu*** *ʿalayhi bi-l-adhiyya*, said when the abuse goes on without stopping.

Al-riththān "The Intermittent," sometimes shortened as *al-rithān*, is rain separated by periods of stillness no shorter than an hour and no longer than one day and night.

[DUST CLOUDS]

Al-rahaj "Raised Dust," *al-ghubār* "The Dust Cloud," and *al-qatām* "Black Dust" occur by night or day. ***Arhajat*** *al-arḍ* "The land **became enveloped in raised dust**" is said when *al-rahaj* beleaguers it. ***Aḍabbat*** *al-arḍ* "The land **was covered by a pall**" is also said, and also ***Qatamat*** *al-arḍ* "The land **was darkened by dust.**"

Al-sayyiq "The Driven" is a rainless cloud driven by the wind.

Al-ighḍān "Tedium" is unceasing rain from which there is no relief. It may last all day and night, and even longer.

NAMES OF THUNDER

The word is *raʿd*, pl. *ruʿūd*. ***Raʿadat*** *al-samāʾ* is said when "The sky **thunders**," and *arʿada* means to be thundered at: ***Arʿada*** *l-qawm* "The people **were beset by thunder**" [is said in such a case].[xxvii]

One type of thunder, not very loud, is *al-irzām* "The Lowing." The loudest sound within a single peal of thunder is called its *hazim* "burst" or *tahazzum*, whether the thunder is weak or strong. *Al-qaʿqaʿa* "The Clatter" is for loud claps of thunder in succession. Heavy thunder is called *al-rajs* and *al-rajsān* "The Very Loud."[xxviii]

Fire that falls from heaven with a loud burst of thunder is called *al-ṣāʿiqa* "The Thunderbolt," pl. *al-ṣawāʿiq*. Thunder heard from a distance is called *al-azīz* "The Resonant," and *al-rizz*○ "The Rumble" is similar to it. A poet said (meter: *rajaz*):

Jāratanā min wābilin a-lā slamī
a-lā slamī usqīti ṣawba d-diyami
ṣawba rabīʿin bākirin lam yanami
***yurazzu razzan** min warāʾi l-akami*
***rizza** r-rawāyā bi-l-mazādi l-muʿṣami*

"Nextdoor raincloud, come and yield!
Come let splash the rain you're holding,
a rain of spring to be our stintless blessing."
Making their rumble heard from behind the hills,
the water-bearers **rumble** of their stoppered increase.

Al-jaljala "The Jingle" is said for the sound of thunder that comes when clouds are blown in from the south, and *al-tahazzuj* "The Trill" is similar to it. *Al-zamzama* "The Murmur" is the most pleasant-sounding of the thunders, and the surest harbinger of rain. *Al-irnān* "The Plaint" is a roar of thunder undivided into separate reports.

○ *AL-RIZZ* is used of sounds that come from an unseen source, two in particular. One is thunder, whether loud or soft. The other is a rumble of the gut, specifically "the noise that accompanies the need to defecate" (*Lisān* art. √*rzz*). By ʿAlī b. Abī Ṭālib (d. 40/661) it was decreed that the worshipper who experiences abdominal *rizz* during prayer should go back and re-perform the ritual ablutions, even if no actual defecation has taken place. The droning buzz of locusts is called *al-razz*.

The word is *barq*, pl. *burūq*. ***Baraqat** al-samāʾ* is said when "The sky **sheds lightning**," and *abraqa* means to be harrassed by it: ***Abraqa** l-qawm* "The people **were beset by lightning**" [is said in such a case].

Al-takashshuf "Full Disclosure" and *al-istiṭāra* "The Outspreading" are said of lightning whose illumination fills the sky.[xxix] *Lamʿ* and *lamʿān* "Fluorescence" are multiple flashes of lightning in succession; seen from far away, this is called *lamḥ* and *lamḥān* "The Glow." *Al-tabassum* "The Chuckle" of lightning is like *al-takashshuf*.[xxx] *Al-istīqād* "The Kindling" is a prolonged series of flashes in rapid succession. The first flash seen is *al-īshām*○ "The First Display." *Al-silsila* "The Chain" is lightning by day, and *al-qurād* "The Wooly" (?) is faint lightning in the rain.[xxxi] A poet said (meter: *rajaz*):

> *Tarabbaʿat wa-d-dahru ʿanhā ghāfilu*
> *āthāra aḥwā barquhu **salāsilu***
>
> Beyond the ken of fate, [the beasts] pastured themselves
> on the leavings of dark clouds whose lightning comes in **chains**.

Lightning that is *khullab* "Deceitful" brings no rain with it. *Al-khafaqān* "The Flutter" is lightning that goes on in succession.[xxxii] *Al-khafw* "The Furtive Gleam" of lightning is when you see it indistinctly from far away. This is the

○ *AL-ĪSHĀM* is "to display a mark," and it is analogous to the above-mentioned seasonal rain called *wasmī*. While *al-wasmī* marks the earth with vegetation, *al-īshām*'s mark is made in the sky, or in the beholder's vision as an afterimage. According to *Lisān* art. √*wshm*, "*Awshamat al-arḍ* 'The earth displayed a mark' is said when plants are first seen sprouting in it, and *Awshamat al-samāʾ* 'The sky displayed a mark' is said when lightning begins to flash."

faintest lightning that can be seen. And *al-wamīḍ* "The Flicker" is weak lightning.

Al-sanā "The Glare" of lightning and its *ḍawʾ* "Illumination" are what you see when you do not see the lightning strike, or when you see it at the moment it emerges.[xxxiii] *Al-sanā* never happens by day, only at night, whether it is clear or cloudy, and for *al-ḍawʾ* the same is true. *Tas͟haqquq* "Forking" names the action of lightning when it fans out from a single filament, and *taʿalluq* "Spreading" is like it. *Takalluḥ* "Rictus" is for persistent lightning, and its repeated flashing in a white-fronted cloud. *Talaʾluʾ* "Pearlescence" is said for strokes of lightning that are not too heavy but follow in rapid succession. *Al-maṣʿ* "The Lash" and *al-ramḥ* "The Kick" are the same thing: light, swift strokes of lightning occurring close together. *Al-ilhāb* "The Flare-Up" of lightning is its quick repetition and overlapping, such that no pause intervenes between its strokes. *Al-ʿarrāṣ*○ "The Light Show" is lightning whose glow is unabating, unlike *al-tabassum* [which is intermittent]. And *al-fary* "The Lengthwise Split" is for the brilliance of the lightning as it hangs in the sky.

NAMES OF CLOUDS

The word is *saḥāba*, pl. *saḥāb*. *Al-g͟haym* "haze" is similarly said, whether the clouds are few or many. *Al-g͟hamām* are "bright white clouds," commonly described as *al-g͟harrāʾ* and *al-g͟hurr* "The Blazes."[xxxiv] *Al-muzn* also are white

○ *AL-ʿARRĀṢ* is defined in *K. al-ʿAyn* as "the cloud that emerges from on high, then descends until it is like a roof, and is not called *ʿarrāṣ* unless it has thunder and lightning in it."[xxxv] This definition connects with *ʿarṣ*, which is "a beam placed over a walled enclosure in order to roof it, over which shorter pieces of wood are laid." As a name for this type of cloud, *al-arrāṣ* would be "The Roofing."

clouds.[xxxvi] *Al-ḥammāʾ* "The Reddish Black" is a black cloud.[xxxvii] *Al-sayyiq* [mentioned above as an epithet for the rainless cloud] is said for clouds set moving by the wind, whether or not they carry water. Any cloud expected to give rain may be called *al-khaliq* "The Sure Thing."

Al-ṣabīr "The Upward-Rearing" is a white cloud you see reared high, as if stacked upon itself.[xxxviii] *Al-sudd* "The Obstruction" is a dark cloud that can arise out of any quarter. A poet said (meter: *wāfir*):○

Tabaṣṣar hal tarā alwāḥa barqin
awāʾiluhu ʿalā l-Afʿāti qūdu
qaʿadtu la-hu wa-s͟hayyaʿanī rijālun
*wa-qad kat͟hura l-mak͟hāyilu wa-**s-sudūdu***

"Look! Do you see the blades of lightning
sparking up and making straight for al-Afʿāh?"
With my retinue of men, I sat to watch the clouds
as they multiplied and **blocked the sky**, betokening rain.

○ This anonymous pair of verses is the only lightning-scene adduced by Abū Zayd in the *Book of Rain.* Several prose examples are presented in the Introduction and endnotes to *jārr al-ḍabuʿ* and *al-mut͟hʿanjir*, but the motif's native medium is poetry. Often, rain-description begins with the poet's address to his companions of the road, urging them to wake up and take notice of the storm.[xxxix] Once alerted, these addressees fade into the background, or perhaps it's better said that they merge with the poem's hearers. After that, human beings disappear from the scene, and the focus shifts to the impact on wildlife, the movements of groundwater, and the vegetative growth that follows. Altogether, it is an exercise in representing the earth's alteration by the sky, putting the poet's powers of simile and description to a rousing test. With few exceptions, the scene begins with lightning.

Like the rain it heralds, lightning can be coefficient to nostalgia and longing.[xl] Perhaps this is because lightning is a natural figure for bridging the divide between monadic entities.[xli] Some lightning-scenes include a prayerlike message to a loved one who is absent.[xlii] Evanescent, breathtaking, and often deadly, lightning is heaven's signature on earth, and the only visible thing as fast as thought.

Al-ʿāriḍ "The Cloudbank" is a cloud seen taking up one side of the sky.[xliii] *Al-jilb* "The Saddle Timber" (?)○ is similar to it but more distant, and thinner than *al-ʿāriḍ*. Also, *al-ʿāriḍ* is white cloud, while *al-jilb* is darker in color. Another type of cloud is *al-naḍad* "The Heaped-Up Goods," which is similar to *al-ṣabīr*, and so is *al-rukām*[xliv] "The Cumulus," which is heaped on top of itself like *al-naḍad*. *Al-rabāb* "The Bunched Clouds" are soft, dark clouds appearing against a cloudy background, but they cannot be called *al-rabāb* unless there is rain. And the first part of a cloud to release its rain is *al-rayyiq*. *Al-kanahwar* "The Imposing Figure" is a huge white cloud. [*Kanahwar* can also be used adjectivally, as when] one speaks of "an **imposing** mass of cloud" (*ghamāma* ***kanahwara***), or "haze **in an imposing mass**" (*ghaym* ***kanahwar***). *Al-ṭakhāʾ* "The Gloom" is a thin layer of cloud. *Al-qazaʿ* "The Tatter" is small and disunited. *Al-namir*, sg. *al-namira* "The Leopardine" is haze with gaps in it that appear as spots.[xlv] Similar to it is *al-jafl* "The Scud," which is any wind-driven cloud that has already spilled its water. And *al-jahām* "The Downcast" is like *al-jafl*.

Abū Zayd said: I heard Ruʾba○ recite:

○ THE SADDLE TIMBER (?) *Lisān* art. √*jlb* reports some disagreement over whether *al-jilb* is the camel-saddle in its entirety, or one of its component parts, or its cover. It would be natural to envision *al-jilb* as a cover when the word is applied to cloud, but the long, thin cloud described here might be thought to resemble a wooden rail of the camel-saddle's frame.

○ The poetry of RUʾBA B. AL-ʿAJJĀJ (d. 145/762) is frequently encountered in *Lisān* and other dictionaries, where it is quoted with such brevity that little of its vitality shines through. His place in literary history is at least secure: along with his father al-ʿAjjāj (d. 97/715), he brought the monorhymed *rajaz* poem to its highest point of development.[xlvi]

As a transmitter of Prophetic hadith, Ruʾba's reliability is questioned by some but upheld by many.[xlvii] His deviations from standard Qurʾānic recitation, in which connection Abū Zayd cites him here, are noted elsewhere.[xlviii] *Lisān* art. √*jfl* says this case owes to the absence of the verb *jafaʾa* "to froth" from Ruʾba's Tamīmī dialect.

> *...fa-ammā z-zabadu fa-yadhhabu* ***jufālan***
> "Foam is what passes away, like **the scud**."

[which is a unique variant of *Sūrat al-Raʿd* (Thunder) 13:17:

> *...fa-ammā z-zabadu fa-yadhhabu* ***jufāʾan***
> "Foam is what passes away, like **the froth**."]○

—meaning that the wind blows it away.

Another kind of cloud is *al-ṣurrād* "The Drifter," which is like *al-jafl*, as are *al-rahaj* and *al-sayyiq* [above]. *Al-ḥabiyy*○ "The Mound Former" is cloud that comes out raining and is slow to leave the sky. The long, mountainous clouds of blazing white that come out over the sea between autumn and spring are called *banāt makhr* "Daughters of the Furrowing of the Sea."[xlix] *Al-zibrij*○ "The Chintz" is like *al-rahaj* and *al-sayyiq* also. *Al-ʿamāʾ*○ "The Lenticular" looks like smoke, and clings to the tops of high peaks. *Al-ḍabāb* "The Pall" is smokelike mist that

○ LIKE THE FROTH: These words are from the fourth verse following *Sūrat al-Raʿd*'s namesake verse.[l] In this visionary passage, the detritus carried by surging groundwaters is likened to dross that collects at the surface of molten metals.[li]

○ *AL-ḤABIYY*'s semantic flexibility is noted by Hussein (2009), 198–99. Its root-verb means "to come near" and "come low"; said of an infant, it means "to crawl." And *Lisān* art. √*ḥbā* notes that when said of blowing sand, *ḥabā* means for it "to pile up."[lii] When it comes to clouds, this secondary meaning seems coeval with the first, insofar as what hugs the ground as it travels may be said to form a mound.[liii]

○ *AL-ZIBRIJ* is a word for frivolity of ornament, elsewhere defined as thin, reddish clouds of doubtful rain.

○ *AL-ʿAMĀʾ* derives from √*ʿmy*, the root of words for "blindness," but this meaning for *ʿamāʾ* is sharply rejected by Abū ʿUbayd al-Qāsim b. al-Sallām (d. 224/838). It is heard in hadith that *al-ʿamāʾ* was once the residence of God.[liv]

covers the sky. The foremost part of an overhanging cloud is called *ẓulla* "a canopy." *Al-ṭakhārīr* are small clouds; their singular form is *ṭukhrūr* "The Wisp."

About *al-ghayāya*, the Arabs disagree: some say it is the cloud itself, when really it is the cloud's shadow. And some call it *al-ghayāʾa*. Kuthayyir ʿAzza[lv] said (meter: *ṭawīl*):

ka-sāʿin ilā ẓilli ***l-ghayāʾati*** *yabtaghī*
maqīlan fa-lammā an atāhā ḍmaḥallati[lvi]

... like one who craves the shade of **a cloud's shadow**,
hastens for it, and gets there just when it dissipates.

In the dialect of Kilāb [this last word is pronounced with /m/ and /ḍ/ reversed]: *amḍaḥallat.*

Al-mukfahirr○ "The Glowering" is a huge cumulus cloud. The word can also serve as an epithet for the dust cloud. Said of haze, *al-ṭurra* "The Fringe" is its farthest visible extremity; *ṭurra* is also said for the edges of a meadow, or bangs of hair. *Al-nashāṣ* "The Lofty," sg. *al-nashāṣa*, are tall white clouds that arise mostly in advance of *al-ʿayn*, and *al-ʿayn* "The Water-Source"[lvii] is said of the cloud that appears from the direction of the *qibla*.○

○ *MUKFAHIRR* (according to *Lisān* art. √*kfhr*) describes a face that is "thick-skinned, thin of flesh, and devoid of affect." Or it is "a thick face, dusty in color," or "a scowling face," or "a face with clenched features and no gaiety in it." It is an epithet of the lion and the steep, stony mountain. It is an active participle, and its verb, *ikfaharra*, is likewise heard in cloud and rain descriptions.[lviii]

○ THE *QIBLA* is the beeline from the Kaʿba to any worshipper's location, and the direction the worshipper faces in prayer. From the perspective of Basra, where Abū Zayd lived, and from the Najdi territories of his informants, the *qibla* coincides with the direction taken by the raincloud called *al-ʿayn*, from over the Red Sea.[lix]

Great or small, a river is called *al-nahr* and *al-nahar*; *al-anhār* is its plural. *Al-jadāwil*○ "canals," sg. *al-jadwal*, are rivulets made to split off from a river to irrigate crops and palm groves.[lx] *Al-qanā*○ "an aqueduct" is a canal made to flow underground, and is not called *qanā*, pl. *aqnāʾ* (or, as some say, *qanāt*, pl. *quniyy*) unless it has a covering.[lxi] Any uncovered watercourse is a *jadwal*, and a *khudad* "channel" is similar to it. All three words are used whether they run dry or flow with water.

Al-kurr is a "holding pool" where water accumulates.[lxii] (The rope that men loop around the trunk of a palm in order to climb it is called *al-karr*.)

To describe water as *laʿīn* "sordid" is to find fault with it. *Al-ʿudmul*, pl. *al-ʿadāmil*, is "well-aged" water, and anything else that is old.[lxiii] Water that does not cover the ankle is described as *ḍaḥl* "shallow" and *ḍaḥḍāḥ*○ "superficial." *Al-raqāq* "a thin layer" is used in a similar fashion. *Al-barḍ* is a "meager" amount of water that you manage to gather, and verb *tabarraḍa* means "to seek water."

○ *AL-JADĀWIL* can be said for natural riverine formations (including blood vessels), but usually it means man-made canals. Later, the graphological meaning of "tabular notation" accrued to this word. What English calls *columnar* arrangement of information is called in Arabic after a *canal*.[lxiv]

○ *AL-QANĀ*, a cognate of Hebrew *qāneh* (and the New Testament place-name *Cana*), is both a *canal* and a length of *cane*. The Latin words for cane (*canna*) and canal (*canalis*) are likely borrowings from the same Semitic root.

○ *ḌAḤL* AND *ḌAḤḌĀḤ* describe "shallow" pools of water. Both go back to √*ḍḥḥ*, a root that is used for the impact of the sun upon the ground. *Al-ḍiḥḥ* is a piece of ground that catches the sun, or it is sunshine itself. To call a body of water *ḍaḥḍāḥ* or *ḍaḥl* is to say it runs no deeper than what the sun touches.[lxv]

Porous rock from which water can be recovered is called *mushāshat al-māʾ* "a water socket," and soft stone that can be dug into is called *hirshamm*. A poet said (meter: *rajaz*):

> ***Hirshammatun** fī jabalin **hirshammi***[lxvi]
> *tabdhulu li-l-jāri wa-li-bni l-ʿammi*
> *wa-l-jānibi l-mudaffaʿi l-mulammi*
>
> In **soft stone**, you are **a soft touch**,
> giving freely to neighbors and to cousins,
> and to the abject and the wronged.

Al-ḥashraj "cavitation" is porous rock below the ground, though some authorities define it as a *ḥisy*○ "aquifer" with a pebbly bottom.

The verb *rashaḥa yarshaḥu* is used when an excavated shaft "sweats" at the first touch of water. *Nashaḥa yanshaḥu* is said of a waterskin, a vessel, or a tract of land that "yields little water," and *nashifa yanshafu*[lxvii] is said when things are "drying up."

The verb *ṭamā yaṭmū* is said of a well that "brims"; *bāthiq* "bursting" has the same meaning, and is said of wells, rivers, and abundant bodies of water. *Baḍīḍ* "seepage" is a small quantity of water exuded from the earth or from a waterskin.

○ *ḤISY* is a word used throughout this section but never defined. It names a geologic feature crucial to human survival in the Arabian Peninsula. As described by Erich Bräunlich: "The subterranean reservoirs called *ḥisy*, *ḥashraj*, [and] *kurr* are of peculiar importance for the stretches of volcanic rock beds, the Ḥarra. They were formed in the recent geologic period of the eruption of volcanic matter which produced the broad lava fields of Arabia. They consist of cavities in strong watertight rock ... covered with a stratum of soft earth, sand or pebble of about one cubit in thickness. This soft covering absorbs the rain or wādī water and conducts it to the rock. Here the one prevents the water from flowing farther and the other from evaporating."[lxviii]

An area that retains water is called *al-masāk* "a catchment," and *al-aḍaʾa* is a lowland pool.[lxix] *Al-samala* "dregs" is residue that water leaves behind.

Al-makhāḍa "a ford" is water that can be crossed by horse or camel or on foot. A canal is called *al-jadūd* "a lactator" only when it holds water, and the same goes for *al-khalīj* "a gulf." *Al-sayḥ* "a stream" is running water from a river or a spring, and the branching canal that distributes it among the crops and palms is called *falaj*○ "an irrigation network."

A poet said (meter: *rajaz*):

Yanshaḥna min Washḥā qalīban ***sukkā***
taṭmū idhā l-wirdu○*ʿalayhā ltakkā*

They drink their fill at a **narrow shaft** of Washḥāʾ
whose level rises when thronged by water-seekers.

Al-sukk is the narrow shaft of a well, from its highest part to its lowest. A well containing lots of water is said "to have its mouth full" (*talaqqama*).

When a waterskin, a trough, a pond, or a vessel is less than half full, but no more than two-thirds empty, the quantity it contains is called *al-rafaḍ* "a remain-

○ *FALAJ*: Cognates of this word occur as place-names across the Middle East.[lxx] The verb *falaja* means "to divide," as when one canal is made to branch from another. (Hebrew *peleg* is likewise a "canal" and a "division.") *Falaja* also means "to part the soil," as with a plow, and land made ready for sowing is called *fallūja*. But Falluja in Iraq derives its name (through Syriac *Pallūgtha*) from *Pallukkatu*, a Neo-Babylonian canal dug westward from the Euphrates River.[lxxi] Assuredly, these all go back to the same Proto-Semitic root.

○ *WIRD* is the verbal noun of *warada yaridu*, meaning "to be present," and more specifically "to be present *at a water-source*." *Wird* therefore names the action of arriving at water, and is also used as a collective noun to mean the arrivers themselves, whether beasts, birds, or human beings.[lxxii]

der," and may be called *al-khibṭ* or *al-khabīṭ* "a small quantity of water" [or "water trampled by beasts"]. A poet said (meter: *rajaz*):

In taslami d-Dafwāʾu wa-ḍ-Ḍarūṭu
yuṣbiḥ la-hā fī ḥawḍihā ***khabīṭu***

When Dafwāʾ and Ḍarūṭ○ get free,
they leave behind a trough of **trampled water**.

Malignant, stale-tasting water is described as *ajin* "gone bad." *Muʿarmiḍ* "scummy" and *muṭaḥlib* "slimy" refer to the green stuff [called *ʿarmaḍ* and *ṭuḥlub*] that rises from the water's bottom until it coats the surface.[lxxiii]

A well that causes people to lose consciousness is called *mūsina* "dizzying," and the fainting spell that people suffer from its water's noxious fumes is called *al-wasn*. This is how most Kilābīs say it, but some of them say *al-asan*, as in ***Asina*** *l-rajul* "The man **fainted.**"[lxxiv] Rainwater staled by camels has become *maṭrūq* "pissed in." *Al-rajʿ* is a "recurrent" pool of groundwater, smaller than the pool called *al-nahy* or *al-nihy* "a ban" [against groundwater's seeping away].

The *khasf*○ of a well is where its water enters in, and is also called its *kawkab*○

○ *DAFWĀ* AND *ḌARŪṬ* mean "Long-Neck" and "Gas Bag," and where these anonymous verses are quoted in *Lisān* art. √*khbṭ*, they are explained as names of camels.

○ *KHASF* is a verbal noun for the well-digger's task of chiseling through a stratum of rock.[lxxv] Here it is an operative feature of the well, namely the pore through which water enters and fills it up.

○ *KAWKAB* is a word for fixed stars, wandering planets, and by analogy, any brilliant thing against a dark background. The flowers of a garden are its *kawkab*, and so is the gleam in a person's eye. A well-built boy with a beautiful face is the *kawkab* of his group (cf. English *cynosure*). As a synonym for *khasf*, it seems a case of synesthesia, where the water's point of entry into the well is named as a gleam in the unlit depths.[lxxvi]

"star." A well that falls into disrepair and disuse after its water dwindles is called *ʿūrān* "blind-eyed" and *tarīka* "forsaken."

The first water to flow [from a newly-excavated well] is called *al-qarīḥa.*[lxxvii] Before that, when the flow is nigh and the dirt grows moist, ***Ittalajat*** *al-rakiyya* "The well **gave ingress**" [is said]. After *al-qarīḥa*, the well is in flow.○ Water that is *sākir* "inebriate" is stagnant water with no current.

Al-ghiṭāʾ is the "lid" you put on a hard-sided vessel, and the "cover" you place over a well, be it a stone or a board. The dirt you cast on top of a lidded well for the purpose of concealment is called *ghibāʾ* "a dummy."[lxxviii] And when you cast dirt into a well without putting a stone or a board over it, it's called *al-dafn* "a burial." The act of placing a lid on a hole in the ground, be it small or large, and then burying it under dirt is called *taghbiya* "dummying" and *taghtiya* "covering." The act of doing so without a lid is called *al-dafn* and *al-taʿwīr* "putting an eye out." Of all these words, only *taghtiya* is additionally said for the act of putting a lid on a vessel.

Al-ranaq "murk" is water with a heavy admixture of clay.[lxxix] *Al-kadar* "turbidity" is like it. The verb *naḍaba* "to run dry" is a synonym of *nashifa* [mentioned above]. *Al-baḍīḍ* "seepage" [also mentioned above] is the action of water when it accumulates slowly, and *al-naḍīḍ* "welling up" is like it.

"Drinkable" water is described as *ʿadhb*. The sweetest and most drinkable of waters is described as *zulāl* "limpid." Similar to *zulāl* is *nuqākh* "thirst-beating," and another name for what is drinkable is *furāt* "sweetwater." Cold water, be it drinkable or briny, is described as *shabim* "frigid," and *qāris* is said for any beverage that is freezing cold.

○ FLOW: Another water-word that Abū Zayd uses without defining it is *nabaṭ*, being the "flow" of a well and hence the well-digger's goal. This idea is at the root of an ethnonym with different connotations in different periods. The Nabataeans were so called long before Islam, for their adroitness at digging after water.[lxxx]

Undrinkably salty water is called *milḥ* "brine." "Putrid" water whose taste cannot be tolerated is called *zuʿāq*. Salty water that is still drinkable is called *mukhḍim* "mouth-filler," and may be described as *khafīj* "potable." *Al-muʿalqim* "colocynthine" is the bitterest water that there is. Water that is *ghalīẓ* "rough" is like *al-mukhḍim*. There is no water more saline and malignant than *al-quʿāʿ* "badwater," and water that is *ujāj* "caustic" is like it.[lxxxi] A poet said (meter: *rajaz*):

Yashrabna māʾan sabikhan ***ujājā***
law yalaghu dh-dhiʾbu bi-hi mā ʿājā
lā yataʿayyafna ***l-ujāja*** *l-mājā*

Swampy and **caustic** is the water that they drink.
A wolf that lapped it would not linger,
but they feel no disgust at salty ***ujāj***.

Waligha yalaghu [heard in the second line] is a verb of drinking, for a canine.

Water described as *imiddān* is "hypersaline."[lxxxii] *Al-ṣarā* is "long-confined" water that has gone bad. *Al-wātin* "pulsing" describes a perpetual water-source that never dwindles. *Al-nazūr* is a "paltry" amount of water, or of anything else. *Al-rawāʾ* is a "large supply" of water.

An abandoned well whose water has gone bad is called *al-sidām* "a stoppage." *ʿŪrān* ["blind-eyed," mentioned above] is used to describe caved-in, tumbled-down wells in both the singular and the plural.

Any river may be called *baḥr* "a sea," but the affiliated verb *istabḥara* "to become sea-like" is reserved for drinkable waters and wells that turn to brine. Water of a higher degree of turbulence than *kadar* is called *ṭamil* "mud." *Al-ḥamʾa*[lxxxiii] is dark [clay] with a rotten odor, and *al-ghiryan*[lxxxiv] is the name of clay carried by rushing water across the surface of the earth and left there, whether it is desiccated or still moist.

The end.

God be praised for His blessing, and prayers be upon His Prophet, our master Muḥammad.

من كل ماء ويقال للبئر المتروكة حين تأجن
اجونا سدام وجماعها السدم ويقال للركيه
التي قد تهدمت وتحفرت عوران وكذلك
الجميع ٥ وقالوا الأنهار كلها بحار والنهر
بحر ويقال للماء اذا غلظ بعد عذوبة قد
استبحر واستبحرت بيركم اذا غلظ ماؤها
ويقال ماء طمل وهو اشد خثرا من الكدر
طمل الماء طملا والحماة السوداء المتغيرة
الريح خبثت الركية تحما حما والغرين الطين
الذي يحمله السيل فيبقى على وجه الارض رطبا
كان او يابسا ٥٥٥

تم الكتاب

والحمد لله على نعمه وصلى الله على نبيه سيدنا محمد
وآله وسلم

NOTES TO **THE BOOK OF RAIN**

[i] This opening section on asterisms and seasons is repeated word for word in a text called *K. al-Azmina wa-talbiyat al-Jāhiliyya* (The Book of Seasons and Invocations of the Pre-Islamic Period), 24–25. Its author, Quṭrub (d. 206/821), was a younger contemporary of Abū Zayd's who is not counted among his students. Abū Zayd's list is assuredly the earlier account, as made clear in Quṭrub's introduction: "And this is another account, on the authority of the tribesmen of Qushayr." Qushayr is another "northern" tribal group of Central Arabia, but the *Qushayriyyīn* (قشيريين) in Quṭrub's text is a scribal misreading of Abū Zayd's *Qaysiyyūn* (قيسيون).

[ii] Allen (1899), 307.

[iii] Kunitzsch (1961), 23–24.

[iv] Allen (1899), 254.

[v] Kunitzsch (1961), 45.

[vi] Rapoport and Savage-Smith (2014), 638.

[vii] Ibn Qutayba, *Adab al-kātib*, 92.

[viii] MacDonald (1992), 1–2.

[ix] "Moderate" in temperature are the nights of this season, if *muʿtadilāt* (with unpointed *dāl*, د) is read in manuscript at 2r5. A note in the margin contests this reading, saying: "*Muʿta<u>dh</u>ilāt*, with pointed letter <u>*dh*</u>*āl* (ذ) is the only correct reading." *Al-muʿta<u>dh</u>ilāt*, however, are defined as days and nights of intense heat during the rising of Canopus (*Lisān* art. √*ʿ<u>dh</u>l*), and this cannot be reconciled with the cool of these nights (*barduhā*) that Abū Zayd mentions.

[x] Miller (2017), 7 and (2024), 186.

[xi] In place of *al-ṣayf* (2r8), the manuscript again has *al-qayẓ*. These movements of the two *Simāk*s correspond to those given earlier for *al-ṣayf* and so I have emended it.

xii At *naḍkhuki* (2v12), a marginal note says: "Al-Zaydī [*sic*] transmitted this with a pointed letter *khāʾ* (خ); others have *naḍḥuki*, with an unpointed *ḥāʾ* (ح)." *Naḍkh*, like *naḍḥ*, means "emission of water," and (on the strength of *Sūrat al-Raḥmān* 55:66) it might seem a more forceful spray than the simile calls for—unless the verses are addressed to the poet's long-striving camel (as is likely).

xiii The verb is heard in a stray verse by al-Kumayt b. Zayd al-Asadī (d. 126/743), describing a wildflower bloom with the conventional simile (meter: *ṭawīl*):

Frisked by the flux of every rainsoaker, the hilltops
were left as if traders sold dyed garments to them
—*Dīwān al-Kumayt*, 226, *Lisān* √*khfsh*.

In a story told by Abū Ḥātim al-Sijistānī, the poetry of al-Kumayt reveals a difference of opinion between Abū Zayd and al-Aṣmaʿī. Ostensibly, it was a question of verb forms, but the poet's ethnicity was also at issue, al-Kumayt being no Bedouin but a non-Arab retainer (*mawlā*) of the Banū Asad who got his start as a schoolteacher in Kufa. Where al-Aṣmaʿī objects to this poet *tout court*, Abū Zayd's only concern is for grammar—specifically, the correct use of Ist- and IVth-form verbs, on which subject he produced a whole book (noted in the Introduction). Abū Ḥātim said:

I asked al-Aṣmaʿī: "In your view, can *abraqa* and *arʿada* be used as verbs of threatening?"

"No," he said. "Rather, one uses *baraqa* and *raʿada*" ("to flash with lightning" and "to thunder").

I said to him: "But al-Kumayt said (meter: *kāmil*):

Abriq wa-arʿid ya Yazī-
du fa-mā waʿīduka lī bi-ḍāʾir

Loose your lightning, Yazīd, and let roll your thunder.
To me, your threats are without consequence."

"But this is by a Jurumqānī, whose people are from Mosul," said al-Aṣmaʿī. "For me he's no linguistic resource."

Abū Ḥātim said: I took my inquiry to Abū Zayd al-Anṣārī, who upheld Kumayt's usage. Just then, we were met by a Bedouin pilgrim bound for Mecca, and a group of us wished to put the question to him "Allow me," said Abū Zayd, and did the asking: "How do you pronounce the verbs 'You flash with lightning' and 'you thunder'?"

"Meaning to threaten somebody?" the Bedouin asked. "Yes," said Abū Zayd. "*Tubriqu* and *tur'idu*," the Bedouin answered [voweling them both as IVth-form verbs, as in Kumayt's verse].

I went back to al-Aṣmaʿī, and reported this to him. Thereupon he recited [a verse by the pre-Islamic poet al-Mutalammis al-Ḍubaʿī, meter: *ṭawīl*]:

Idhā jāwazat min Dhāti 'Irqin thaniyyatan
*fa-qul li-Abī Qābūsa mā shi'ta fa-ʿ**rudi***

When [your camel] puts the pass of Dhāt 'Irq behind you, you can
versify all you want about Abū Qābūs, and **threaten him.**

[in which "thunder / threaten" is voweled as a Ist-form imperative].

Al-Aṣmaʿī said to me: "Now that's how Arabic is spoken."
—Abū l-Fatḥ 'Uthmān ibn Jinnī (d. 392/1002), *al-Khaṣā'is* (Special Features [of Language]) III.293–94, cf. Baalbaki (2014), 23, and van Gelder (1988), 98–99.

xiv A connection between the Arabic root $\sqrt{}$*djn* and the ancient Near Eastern god Dagan was hypothesized by Albright (1920), 319n27. As far back as the third millennium BCE, Dagan was a god of the Middle Euphrates region, and in the Iron Age his cult was taken up by the Philistines of Ashdod and Gaza. In some places, he served as a weather god, and in Ugaritic epic (where the storm god Baal is called by the epithet *bn dgn* "Son of Dagan") Albright theorized Dagan was a weather god, too. However, *dgn* has no other weather-associations in Canaanite, nor any meteorological cognates outside of Arabic $\sqrt{}$*djn*, and support for Albright's thesis is wanting; see Feliu (2003), 278–306, and Renfroe (1992), 93–94.

xv As described by Tillier (2006), 140–41, 'Ubayd Allāh al-ʿAnbarī was an authority in multiple disciplines, "including law, poetry, lexicography and tribal genealogy. In matters of jurisprudence he adhered to the old Basran school, of which he is considered a foremost representative. The word most often used to describe him in the biographical literature is *ʿāqil* [sharp-witted]." In theological terms his outlook was broad. Ibn Qutayba says that when two interpretations of a given Qur'ānic verse were diametrically opposed, 'Ubayd Allāh could see validity in both (*Ta'wīl mukhtalif al-ḥadīth*, 45).

His connoisseurship of poetry is also attested. In a lighthearted multigenerational tale from *Aghānī* XII.222, ʿUbayd Allāh is embarrassed by an invective verse that was delivered against his own grandfather. Authentic or not, it depicts an *homme d'esprit* who accepted reproach gracefully.

The story begins in the early Umayyad period, during Ziyād b. Abī Sufyān's governorship of Iraq (45–53/665–673). When the grammarian Abū l-Aswad al-Duʾalī (d. 69/688) sent letters to two of Ziyād's revenue officers, who were Nuʿaym b. Masʿūd al-Nahshalī and Ḥuṣayn b. Abī l-Ḥurr al-ʿAnbarī (grandfather of the future ʿUbayd Allāh), "Nuʿaym fulfilled his hopes for the courtesy of an answer, but Ḥuṣayn pitched Abū l-Aswad's letter over his shoulder. On his messenger's return this was reported to Abū l-Aswad, who composed for Ḥuṣayn this invective poem (meter: *ṭawīl*):

> When my letter came, you thought it begged
> for charity, but my hopes lay in a different direction.
> My messenger informs me that
> your left hand took my letter,
> and with one look at the [return] address, you cast it aside
> like the cast-off, worn-out sole of your shoe.
> Nuʿaym b. Masʿud is worthy of all he receives
> and you are worthy of what's already yours.
> It attacks and advances without awareness or knowledge:
> what is dim-wittedness, if not that?"

As shown in the sequel, two generations later, this last verse became a proverbial expression for stupidity:

> "When a plaintiff got confused in his testimony before ʿUbayd Allah b. al-Ḥasan b. al-Ḥusayn b. Abī l-Ḥurr the judge of Basra, ʿUbayd Allah quoted to him the verse:
>
> He attacks and advances without awareness or knowledge:
> what is dim-wittedness, if not that?
>
> The man said: 'If your honor will allow me to approach, I have something to say.' 'You may,' said ʿUbayd Allah.

"The man said, 'Of all people, it is you who have most reason to keep quiet about that poem, for you know about whom it was spoken.' 'Ubayd Allah grinned and said, 'It is evident to me that you are the wronged party in this case. Return to your home.' He then ordered the defendant to approach and said, 'You are to pay him the full amount demanded.'"

xvi This is the sense in which *waṭaf* (plural of *waṭfāʾ*) is heard in another rain-tableau by Imruʾ al-Qays, recited by the poet Dhū l-Rumma (d. 117/736) when Abū ʿAmr b. al-ʿAlāʾ asked him which poet had best described the rain (meter: *ramal*):

The rain settles in and stays for a nonstop spatter.
Its **beetlings** roundabout compass the land.
When it eases, your tent-pegs jut from the ground.
When it resumes, they are submerged [and can't be seen].
You see the clever lizard work its nimble claws
[like paddles], where there is no dust for it to tread,
and you see the bushes [rising from the flood] like ladies'
covered heads. And that was just the first falling.
An hour of this, and then a downpour takes its side,
wings held low, unable to contain its gushing.
An East Wind drew it off as night was landing,
only for the South to back it up with clouds a-bursting.
Before the rain had peaked, the plains of Khaym,
Khufāʾ and Yusur were cinched by rising floods.
Lean-flanked, strong, and noble was the horse
I rode away on, first thing the next morning.

—*Dīwān Imriʾ al-Qays* II.627–29.

xvii *Jārr al-ḍabuʿ* is heard in a spirited narration of Ibn Durayd's. It is set in the late pre-Islamic period, and recounts a Bedouin nomad's repartee with one of Ḥīra's kings. The nomad's description of the rainstorm is a lightning-scene in rhymed prose, and the dialogue leading up to it is worthy of Cervantes. I set this gem off with its own diamond:

♦

It was reported to me by Abū Ḥātim that Abū ʿUbayda said:

One day, al-Nuʿmān sallied forth after a rainstorm. On meeting with an Arab mounted on a camel, he hailed him, and the Arab obeyed his summons. "How is the land that you have left behind you?" al-Nuʿmān asked.

"Wide and spacious," said the Arab. "With easy lowlands, rugged hills, and mountains firmly rooted, it is a capable sustainer of all that sits on it."

"My question to you was about the skies," said al-Nuʿmān.

"High and free-standing is its sky," the Arab said, "without the aid of poles or tent-cords. Its day and night are clearly separated, and its sun and moon follow each other in succession."

"That's not what I'm asking about!" said al-Nuʿmān.

"Then say what's on your mind," the Arab said.

"Has there been rainfall, and if so can you describe it?"

"Yes," the Arab said. "The rain installed itself over our land for three long stretches. It soaked the ground, left it swampy, and then left it ankle-deep. When I went forth and surveyed the land, I found no part as far as Tiʿshār that was spared. On every side, the clouds dropped showers and boomed out to each other, and heavily the flow drave on, erasing landmarks and filling hollows and uprooting trees. All settled folk kept to their shelters, and no traveler could make a move until the sky quit harrying us with its blessings. When solid land had re-emerged, and pathways through the fields could be descried, I came out to observe the sky and every quarter of its rim. No refuge could I find except for caverns in the hills, for a 'Hyena Driver' had been disgorged: the lowlands were like seas of slapping waves, the rugged hills were wrapped in flotsam, and carcasses of wild animals were flung in all directions. And I have not ceased treading the sky's waters and wading through their residue until my arrival in your land."

—*K. Waṣf al-maṭar*, 55–57; cf. *K. al-Maṭar wa-l-raʿd wa-l-barq wa-l-rīḥ* (The Book of Rain, Thunder, Lightning, and Wind), 58–61 by Ibn Abī l-Dunyā (d. 281/894), and Abū Hilāl al-ʿAskarī, *Dīwān al-maʿānī* II.8–9.

xviii *Iḥtafala*'s occurrence in a rain-description by al-Ḥusayn b. Muṭayr (d. 170/786) is for the moment of rain's materialization in the sky. This is in a celebrated poem improvised on the spot, when (in a report by Abū Zayd's student al-Riyāshī) a patron ordered Ibn Muṭayr to extemporize a description of the rain while it was falling.

Al-Riyāshī said: Abū l-ʿĀliya [al-Shāmī, d. after 240/853] informed me that Abū ʿImrān al-Makhzūmī said:

At Medina, my father and I paid a call on the governor, who was a man of Quraysh, and in attendance on him was Ibn Muṭayr. Just then, an abundant rain began to fall, and the governor told Ibn Muṭayr to describe it. "Let me go up and look at it first," said the poet. After ascending and making his observations, he came down and said (meter: *kāmil*):

The cloud's fill of rainwater caused its teats to burst out,
  and when its milk began to give, those teats gave forth.
Swelling like an udder that is swelling to contain the sky
  was its behemoth of a swelling bag. Underneath it went
low-dipping clouds aflash with lightning that goes before
  the outburst of a long broad-brush of rain.
Its lightning has the force of a hot gust,
  stirring tree limbs in the desert when it strikes.
When heaven's waters **came together**, their burgeoning
  had the appearance of a dingy cloud of dust.
But the cloud laughed with lightning and flowed with tears,
  and that is not how dust clouds operate.
Without sadness and without mirth, its laughter
  blended with its weeping [—when, all of a sudden,]
an errant East Wind kicked up and drove it,
  and then a South Wind with its water-bags all packed,
and then a wind blowing obliquely between
  the cardinal points. Their play with the cloud was unrelenting.
Its liquid mass was that of a sea.
  If other clouds be seas, this one was their sky.
Heavy were its low-bulging parts, and when its side rent
  and gave water, whole tracts of stone turned into rivers.
It is a cloud that traveled to give birth, and so it did
  over the basins, with plenty overflowing
as more clouds, yet to be tapped, come whitely blazing,
  virgins pregnant yet with stores of water.
When they turn dark, they are like charcoal in their blackness.
  When they laugh [with lightning] they are clarity itself.

> If their water were shed over the depths along the coast,
> the depths would have to cast aside their waters.
> —*Shiʿr* I.34–35; *Aghānī* XVI.20; al-Marzūqī,
> *al-Amkina* 333; Yāqūt, *Muʿjam al-udabāʾ* III.1159–60.

xix *Al-murwiya* appears in manuscript (4r12) as *al-murwiyya*. Although Cheikho and Gottheil emend it to *al-murawwiya* (active participle of the IInd-form verb *rawwā* "to irrigate"), *al-murwiya* (active participle of the IVth-form verb *arwā*, with the same meaning) is more likely. Outside the *Book of Rain*, no attestation of either form as a word for rain can be found.

xx *Muthʿanjir* for the cloud is heard in the legendary contest between Jumʿa and Hind bt. al-Khuss, two sisters of the pre-Islamic period who were renowned for their rhetorical gifts. This was set in the Central Arabian market town of ʿUkāẓ, where in order to find out whose gift for descriptive speech was greater, they were quizzed by a character named al-Qalammas al-Kinānī. His first question: "Jumʿa, what kind of he-camel do you love best?" She said:

> "I love the huge and vigorous, the symmetrical and strong of build, its flesh like chiseled marble, dark in color, whose lip dangles pendulously and whose call is heard from far away."
>
> "How does that sound to you, Hind?" al-Qalammas asked.
>
> "For a long and difficult journey through barren wastes, this kind is best. But another he-camel is better loved by me."
>
> "Tell it to me," said al-Qalammas. Hind said:
>
> "I love the one with a lofty neck, compact of build, long on strength and endurance, and little given to complaint as it supports its burden throughout its desert wanderings."

On goes the disputation. What kind of he-camel is most disagreeable? What kind of she-camel is best loved? What kind of mares and stallions, and what kind of goats? And then:

> "Both of you have spoken well," said al-Qalammas. "So what kind of cloud is best in your sight, Jumʿa?" She said:

"I love every dark and coiling cumulus, quivering and dipping so low that with your palm you can practically stand up and stroke it."

"How does that sound to you, Hind?" asked al-Qalammas. She said:

"My sister describes a cloud with slackened spouts, and lots of spattering and copious drawing-off of water. But there is another cloud that I love better."

"Tell it to me, then," said al-Qalammas. Hind said:

"I love every high-rearing, moisture-laden cloud, ripe and plenishing (*muthʿanjir*) with proportionate sides, throwing off lightning like the illumination of a lamp."

—Aḥmad b. Abī Ṭāhir Ṭayfūr (d. 280/893), *Balāghāt al-nisāʾ* (Eloquent Orations by Women), 124–27.

xxi For some authorities, *al-waliyy* was an astral rain period with its own *anwāʾ*, coming after the *wasmī* rain. Varisco (1987), 261, 263.

xxii *Al-wadq* is heard in the Qur'ān at *Sūrat al-Nūr* 24:43 (quoted ahead in the note to *sanā l-barq*), and also in *Sūrat al-Rūm* 30:48:

It is God Who sends the winds and stirs the clouds, and spreads them in the sky however He will. He splits them apart, and you see **the rain encroaching** from their portals. He strikes with it whomever He will among his worshippers, and in that moment they rejoice.

xxiii On *ḍariba*, a marginal note of fol. 5r reports a difference of opinion among Abū Zayd's students, with Abū Ḥātim endorsing it as an epithet for the frost-singed earth and al-Riyāshī discounting this for some reason.

xxiv Soaking dews are common in the Arabian Peninsula's coastal deserts. On a 1947 crossing of South Arabia, Wilfred Thesiger was told by his Rawashid Bedouin guide that dew burns up green plants. *Arabian Sands* (ch. 8), 125.

xxv The expression is heard in a famous poem by the pre-Islamic "brigand poet" (*ṣuʿlūk*) Ta'abbaṭa Sharran:

Along the pass from here to Salʿ
a man lies slain. His blood will not **go unavenged**.

Goethe included a version of this poem in the notes to his *West-östlicher Divan* (1819), where the verse appears: "Unter dem Felsen am Wege / Erschlagen liegt er, / in dessen

Blut / kein Thau herabträuft." On the poem's transmission and translation history, see Heinrichs (2006) and Larcher (2012), 35–91.

xxvi Noted in Sperl and Shackle (1996) II.8. In Arabic as in English, "to moisten a palm" (*nadā l-kaff*) is an expression for generosity as well as bribery; see note xxix ahead for the poem by Wasnā bt. ʿĀmir, where *al-nadā* is translated as "a liberal hand."

xxvii For Abū Zayd's judgment regarding the verbs *arʿada* and *abraqa*, see above note xiii to *al-ḥafsha*.

xxviii Alongside these names for the roar of thunder appears the marginal note: "Abū Zayd informed us on the authority of ʿAmr b. ʿUbayd, on the authority of al-Ḥasan [al-Baṣrī], that the Prophet said: 'Thunder is the angel in charge of clouds, and when you hear its voice, it is praising God (*Al-raʿdu malakun muwakkalun bi-l-saḥābi wa-tasbīḥuhu ṣawtuhu lladhī tasmaʿūna*).'"

The externality of this hadith to the *Book of Rain* was discussed in the Introduction. An exegesis of it would begin with short biographies of the hadith's transmitters ʿAmr b. ʿUbayd (d. ca. 144/761) and Ḥasan al-Baṣrī (d. 110/728), both of them hugely important figures in the intellectual history of Islam. It would also require an excursus on al-Muʿtazila, the religious movement of which ʿAmr was a founding principal. The Muʿtazila were the first to apply Greek logic and dialectic to the interpretation of Islamic scripture and hadith, inventing Islamic theology (*kalām*) in the process. This at any rate describes their activities at Baghdad in the later second/eighth century; the present hadith shows a receptivity to fabulous cosmology not readily associated with the later movement.

ʿAmr's relationship to Ḥasan is fundamental to al-Muʿtazila's history. Supposedly, the movement's name commemorates the "withdrawal" (*iʿtizāl*) by ʿAmr and Wāṣil b. ʿAṭāʾ (d. 131/749) from Ḥasan's study group at Basra. Whether this took place in Ḥasan's lifetime, or was a reaction against his successor Qatāda b. Diʿāma (d. 117/735), depends on whose account you read. At issue mainly was the doctrine of free will, which the Muʿtazilites deemed a necessary precondition for judgment by a just God. Meanwhile, predeterminism remained an article of faith among Ḥasan's mainstream inheritors, from whom it passed into Sunni orthodoxy.

ʿAmr's relationship to Ḥasan was therefore something partisans of orthodoxy were keen to discount (Mourad 2006, 50). Abū Zayd's narration of the hadith on ʿAmr's authority signals his own Muʿtazilite sympathies, though its content touches no point of controversy. Aḥmad b. Ḥanbal, who was tortured for his anti-Muʿtazilite convictions, relates the same hadith (*Musnad* IV.284–86), as does the later Muʿtazilite Jār Allāh al-Zamakhsharī (d. 538/1144) in his Qur'ānic commentary *Kashshāf ḥaqā'iq al-tanzīl* (Revealer of the True Realities of Revelation) IV.353, in reference to *Sūrat al-Raʿd* (Thunder) 13:12–13.

Al-Tirmidhī (d. 279/892) relates the hadith on the authority of Ibn ʿAbbās (d. 68/687), to the effect that Muḥammad was approached by a group of Jews, who peppered him with questions of natural philosophy. "Tell us about the thunder," said one of them. "What is it?"

The Prophet responded, "It is one of the angels, the one in charge of clouds, who drives them on with goads of fire wherever God wills."

"Then what's the sound that reaches our ears?" they asked.

"It is the angel's cry (*zajra*) that sets the clouds moving in the direction they're supposed to go," he said.

"You're right!" they said, and the narration ends with their praise for Muḥammad's sagacity.

—Thus in al-Tirmidhī's *al-Jāmiʿ al-Ṣaḥīḥ* (Comprehensive and Reliable Hadith Collection), IV.356–357; also in Ibn Abī l-Dunyā, *K. al-Maṭar*, 113–25 and *K. al-ʿAẓama* (The Book of Majesty), 265–67 by Abū l-Shaykh b. Ḥayyān al-Iṣbahānī (d. 396/1005).

xxix The *takashshuf* of the lightning is described in verses 6–10 of a 35-verse poem by Abū Dhu'ayb al-Hudhalī (d. ca. 28/649), meter: *ṭawīl*:

Let waters pour for Umm ʿAmr while the night lasts.
Let pour black drums of cloud.
If they dwindle, let the East Wind usher
in a wisp, then let the wisp unfurl
and drink up water from the sea, and ride
the bawling wind black-fronted out of Abyssinia,
its lightning's glare as steady as a Jew's lamp, blazing
and disclosing all. While it holds its water

everything is lit, as in a Roman township,
where high-hung lanterns shine while everyone is sleeping.
—Al-Sukkarī, *K. Sharḥ ash'ār al-Hudhaliyīn* (The Book of Commentary on the Poems of the Tribe of Hudhayl) I.128–30; *Dīwān Abī Dhu'ayb* 47–48.

xxx *Al-tabassum* is a "smile" or "laugh." What makes it a metaphor for lightning is the sudden, involuntary exposure of bright teeth. The word is heard in these verses by 'Abīd b. al-Abraṣ (d. ca. 555 CE), whose lightning-scene is followed by a prolonged comparison of the poet's acumen to a fish's talent for swimming. "A peculiar image," remarks the editor of 'Abīd's *Dīwān* (73n10), "like nothing else known to us in Arabic literature" (verses 1–16 of a 24-verse poem, meter: *wāfir*):

Lightning had me sleepless in a strobing,
pearly chain, in piled clouds filled-out
and fecundated. The darkling water-luggers
gushed out their porous sides
and glowered as they scored the earth with
rainfall, scooping the ground.
They came together, formed a level damper,
and shot out forelocks where their flow spouted,
their sides a lightless shade of gloom
as dark as night, or as the sea deep-reaching.
It was as if the asterisms **smiled**
when night rejoiced in flashy brilliance,
showing off what lights up pretty faces
when **laughter** parts the lips of dark-eyed girls.
Ask the poets: Have they swum the seas
of poetry and braved its depths like I have?
In versecraft solemn and satiric,
my tongue is nimbler than a fish under
the water, expertly plying the surging billow
of the sea whose billows are in violent commotion.

In pursuit or flight, the fish's sides
flash brilliantly with every whip of its tail,
while its spawn dodge for shelter
amid the slick rubble of the sea.
For daughters of water, life is over when you
take them from their element—but no sooner
does a hand try to seize one than it
wriggles free, no matter how sudden the attack,
with a whip and a skip and a viscous getaway. The fish
of the sea is black in color with streaks of pallor,
the sea's own very black hue, with scales that knit
together like pliant armor of shimmering chain.

xxxi *Qurād*, Cheikho notes (12n1), is not a word for "cloud" in any lexicon, and it seems to have confounded al-Marzūqī. Where this passage is quoted in his *K. al-Azmina* (338), *al-qurād* is excised, so that the passage reads: "*Al-silsila* is lightning by day, or lightning during rain, and it is faint lightning."

Their cautions are valid: *qurād* means "tick." But other cloud-words stemming from its root are attested. *Lisān* art. √*qrd* defines *qarid* as a composite cloud "whose surfaces resemble the knotting of woolen hairs." In manuscript (7b2), the word is clearly voweled as *al-qurād*, and there are no grounds for changing it.

xxxii The *takhfāq* of lightning (formed on the same root as *khafaqān*) is mentioned by Mulayḥ b. al-Ḥakam al-Hudhalī, a poet whose life circumstances are all but unknown. Ali Hussein surmises that he participated in the Islamic conquest of Egypt, and dates his *floruit* to the first quarter of the first century of Islam (meter: *ṭawīl*):

Consider the lightning shining out and dying on us
at the end of night, the nonstop flicker
like the **flutter** of a wing. By its light you see
al-Nīr's ridge, and next to it, Ḍariyya's slopes.
Its night-journey is strenuous, and leaves behind
pools in the sand, unslicked by algae.

Its clouds hang low, and irrigate
the rolling hills, and fill up every wadi.
A flock of rails is flushed by the storm.
From their particolored feathers, you see water fly.
I watched it take a southward turn, where Ḥurriyāt
drank pondfuls of it, before the storm continued west.
—*Sharḥ ashʿār al-Hudhaliyīn* III.1050–51.

xxxiii *Sanā l-barq* ("The glare of lightning") is a common phrase, heard in the Qurʾān at *Sūrat al-Nūr* (The Light) 24:43:

Do you not see that God drives on the clouds and then conjoins them, and then He heaps them up? You see the rain incoming from their portals. From mountains in the sky He sends down hail, to strike with it whomever He will, and from whomever He will He averts it. **The glare of His lightning** all but takes away the power to see.

xxxiv *G͟hurr* is an adjective connected to *al-g͟hurra*, which is the white marking on a horse's forehead, called in English a "blaze." As an epithet for *al-g͟hamām*, it is heard in a verse by al-Ḥuṭayʾa (d. after 41/661) quoted in *Lisān* art. √*g͟hmm* (meter: *ṭawīl*):

When you are far from us, there goes our springtime.
Our thirst is quenched by **blazing clouds** when you come back.

xxxv al-Khalīl, *K. al-ʿAyn* III.130 (art. √*ʿrṣ*); Jumʿa (1993), 26.

xxxvi *Muzn* is also a word for "cloud" in general, as in *Sūrat al-Wāqiʿa* (The Event) 56:68–70:

Have you seen the water that you drink? / Are you the ones who send it down from *al-muzn*, or are We its senders? / We could make it caustic-tasting, if We wanted to. Why have you no gratitude?

xxxvii The manuscript (fol. 8v5) has *al-ḥamāʾ*, and as Cheikho notes (13n2) this is not the name of a cloud. The emendation *al-ḥammāʾ* suggests itself instantly, as heard in the cloud-description by Muʿaqqir b. Ḥimār's daughter, quoted on page xxvii of the Introduction.

xxxviii *Al-ṣabīr* occurs in a memorable simile of al-Khansāʾ (d. ca. 23/644), comparing an asymmetrically-pitched battle to merging clouds of uneven size (meter: *mutaqārib*):

How many battalions, helmet-topped
  and mailed in chain, have we walked up to!
Like a wisp of cloud facing **a tall rearing one**
  are we, before the clouds are hurled together.
  —*Dīwān al-Khansāʾ*, 102–3; *Lisān* art. √*ṣbr*.

xxxix The poet is conventionally a man. "[W]omen poets were not generally known for sustained instances of description," notes Hammond (2010), 112, and this includes *waṣf al-maṭar*—with the significant exception of a poem attributed to "a woman of the Banū Asad" (and to a *man* of Asad in Ibn Abī l-Dunyā's *K. al-Maṭar*, 74–75). In one anthology, *K. al-Ashbāh wa-al-naẓāʾir min ashʿār al-mutaqaddimīn wa-al-jāhiliyyati wa-al-mukhaḍramīn* (The Book of Similarities and Resemblances Among the Poetic Works of Early Islam, the pre-Islamic Period, and the Generation Spanning the Two) II.245–46, by the Khālidī brothers Abū Bakr Muḥammad (d. 380/990) and Abū ʿU<u>th</u>mān Saʿīd (d. 390/1000), the woman of Asad is given a name. "Wasnā, the daughter of ʿĀmir al-Asadiyya," it says, and then: "These verses are among the most natural of her tribe's poetic works (*min aṭbaʿ a<u>sh</u>ʿārihim*), with the most peculiar motifs. We know of no description of drought and relief from drought that compares to it."

My translation of Wasnā's poem appeared in a 2017 volume of essays honoring Kathleen Fraser (meter: *mutaqārib*):

We know you saw us wearing out the wells
  when water kept its distance for too long,
shunning its environs all unjustly
  and reducing our catchpools to arid stone,
when from the crowns of thornèd trees there went up
  in whispers to their lord in Heaven secret cries,
and Earth gaped open to the grievances of camels
  re-echoed by the [empty] water-pits.
At night by the wallow we gathered in desperation.
  Our heads were covered and our arms were bare.
"Borrow the right," we said, "to [call your hand]
  a liberal hand, and to the end of your days enjoy

security and freedom! A liberal hand
  may find its gift [to the needy] was but a loan!"
As we braced our insides
  there lit up a spreading bank of cloud,
and then the cloud advanced, no faster than
  a tender, broken-footed camel drive.
Through portals in its outer edges, it laughed
  and sang, and let out stray bursts of tears,
lit by lightning like a lady's sash,
  tied and untied from around her middle.
And as we began to doubt the cloud's salvation,
  fearing lest it fail to claim our turf,
at a commander's gesture from up above it, [meaning]
  "Let it go"—*halumma*—it followed the command.

[xl] Hussein (2009), 37–99; Wagner (2010), 89–92.

[xli] This is how Plato describes his esoteric pedagogy in the *Seventh Letter*, 341cd: "In a flash it is engendered in the soul, like light carried by a leaping spark." Aleida Assmann, who quotes this passage, discusses lightning as a metaphor for memory in Assmann (2011), 162–63, as does Gruendler (2001).

[xlii] Hussein (2009), 227–31.

[xliii] As a word for cloud, *al-ʿāriḍ* (literally, "the broad") occurs in *Sūrat al-Aḥqāf* (The Dunes) 46:24 and its telling of the destruction of ʿĀd, a nation of the past whose response to their approaching doom was to say: "Here we have **a cloudbank** that brings rain" (cited ahead in note 35 to the Appendix).

[xliv] *Rukām* is heard in *Sūrat al-Nūr* 24:43 for the cloud that God "heaps up" (*yajʿaluhu rukāman*), quoted above in note xxxiii.

[xlv] *Al-namira* and *al-namir* are marginal corrections to the manuscript forms *al-namra* (9r14) and *al-nimr* (9v1).

[xlvi] To put it another way, Ru'ba's achievements in monorhymed *rajaz* all but killed the medium for later poets. There is another form called "paired" (*muzdawij*) or "doubled" (*mathnawī*) *rajaz*—rhyming couplets, basically, in which the rhyme changes from couplet

to couplet. This form lends itself to longer compositions, and is better suited for narrative purposes than Arabic qaṣīda form. *Mathnawī* entered Persian as *masnavi*, and became the default medium for Persianate long-form poetry; but Ru'ba's medium of choice was always monorhymed (*mashtūr*) *rajaz*.

A member of the tribe of Tamīm, Ru'ba was highly esteemed by the grammarians of his day. While his panegyric work demonstrates some proximity to political power, his poems also testify that his access to patronage was intermittent. "His verses often complain of poverty," says Hilālī (1982) I.40, "even while alluding to occasional windfalls. His lack of means is stressed in a report by the grammarian Yūnus b. Ḥabīb (d. 182/798), to the effect that Ru'ba would send his son ʿAbd Allāh around to ask his acquaintances for spare change." It also is told of Ru'ba that he made meals of roasted rat. "It's cleaner than poultry," he would tell people. "The rat eats the best of your food and grain stores, while your chickens eat yard waste" (*Shiʿr* II.495–96, *Aghānī* XX.223).

These same acquaintances among the grammarians made habitual recourse to Ru'ba's poetic output, drawn by the abstruseness of his vocabulary and his cultivated rudeness of style. "[H]is poems are among the most difficult in the Arabic language," writes Heinrichs (1995), 577, "as they are full of words that are never or only very rarely found in other poets—one even suspects that, for the sake of effect, the poet coined new words which did not previously exist" (a complaint made against him by Ibn Jinnī in *al-Khaṣāʾis* III.298). Heinrichs continues: "The resulting style is rough, harsh, but forceful, at times willfully obscure, pronouncedly Bedouin-like, a *lingua rustica* [thus Ahlwardt in Ru'ba (1903), xii] which often borders on the grotesque and ironic and seems to acquire the character of a parody of the ancient qaṣīda."

Not only was Ru'ba aware of the grammarians' activities but, as Heinrichs mentions, he positively resented their claim to expertise, as made apparent in his work (lines 135–45 of a 238-line *rajaz* poem):

> Far from my career's end, I am no greenhorn, either.
> My compositions are the work of a master composer.
> Picture me relying on notebooks—propping myself
> on a plucked twig [of words] gone by!
> The grammarian lacks my insight into these things,

no matter how he contorts his face and sets his jaw akilter.
He seems keenly versed, and good at getting his point across,
until [language] rears up in me, effortless, aright.
What appears [to others] behind an inaccessible veil
is subservient [to me]. What I go up against
goes down fast inside my strong encircling rope.

—*Der Dīwān des Reğezdichters Rūba*, 61.

xlvii Ibn Ḥajar al-Asqalānī, *Tahdhīb al-Tahdhīb* (Rectification of the *Rectification*) III.290–91.

xlviii Ru'ba's Qur'ānic readings carried no religious authority, but were perpetuated all the same by Ibn Khālawayh, Ibn Jinnī, and other grammarians (Baalbaki 2014, 94). This particular variant of *Sūrat al-Raʿd* 13:17 is also recorded in the *Gharīb al-ḥadith* (Uncommon Vocabulary of Prophetic Narration) II.448 of al-Bustī (d. 388/998), who cites Abū Zayd's student Abū Ḥātim as his source.

xlix *Banāt Makhr* are a seasonal marker. The sea in question is the Red. Where *banāt makhr* is heard in a poem by Ṭarafa b. ʿAbd (mid-sixth century CE), context shows them to be transient apparitions, fated to disappear around the time of the summer caravans (meter: *ramal*):

The perfume of her mouth, diffused by laughter,
is like a dab of musk in gelid water
chilled by wind and halted in the middle
of a level meadow, before it hits the wadi.
The scraps of debris in the stilled waters
resolve into a floor at the pool's bottom.
High summer's heat is dispelled by the pool's frigidity,
and frigidity is dispelled by her true warmth.
What did you call her? "Summer lounger"? "A woman
short on issue"? Don't upbraid me, nor
compare her to **the daughters of the furrowed waters**
that droop like lanky leaves in summer.

Let my castigator be her gentle, perfumed voice
on the day I get the news of her departure.
—*Dīwān Ṭarafa b. ʿAbd*, 66–68, *Lisān* art. √*mkhr*.

Lisān's entry also carries a report by the grammarian Abū ʿAlī al-Fārisī (d. 377/987) on the theory of his teacher Ibn al-Sarrāj (d. 316/928), which was that *makhr*'s initial consonant was the result of a phonetic shift from /*b*/ to /*m*/, and that *makhr* therefore relates to *bukhār* "water vapor." Al-Fārisī's lack of confidence in the theory is tactfully expressed.

ⁱ Tradition accounts for the revelation of *Sūrat al-Raʿd* with the following story. At Medina, there came to the Prophet a delegation of the Banū ʿĀmir headed by a villain named ʿĀmir b. al-Ṭufayl, who proposed a deal. In exchange for ʿĀmir's conversion to Islam, Muḥammad would acknowledge ʿĀmir's rule over the nomadic Arabs of the desert, while ʿĀmir would acknowledge Muḥammad's control of the towns, thus dividing political control over all Arabia between them. Upon the Prophet's refusal, one version has it that ʿĀmir and a confederate named Arbad b. Qays made a fumbling attempt on his life, and that both men lost their lives shortly afterward, Arbad to a stroke of lightning. (Thus narrated by Ibn Kathīr in *The Life of Muḥammad* IV.76–81; for a different view of Arbad, see ahead note lxiii to *al-ʿudmul*.)

This tradition holds that *Sūrat al-Raʿd* 13:12–13 was revealed in commemoration of Arbad's death. But it is not necessary to know the story to appreciate *Sūrat al-Raʿd*'s invocation of the thunder:

> It is He who makes you see the lightning, and feel fear or hope from it. It is He who generates the heavy clouds. / The **thunder** sings its praise of Him, as do the angels, out of fear. He sends out bolts to strike whomever He will, in the middle of their disputations over God. Punishingly deliberate is He.

ⁱⁱ The standard reading of *Sūrat al-Raʿd* 13:17 goes like this:

> He sends down water from the sky, and the wadis flow with it as best they can, and the flow bears away the swelling foam. And in [the crucible] that is held over fire in hopes of [forging] jewelry or hardware, there is foam like it. This is God's emblem for the distinction between truth and vanity. **Foam is what passes away, like the froth.** The benefit to humanity in the earth has not been swept away. God coins similitudes like these [as instructive emblems].

Thematically, the verse belongs in the Book of Waters. But Abū Zayd's concern here is for *jufal* and *jufā'*. In all the *Book of Rain*, it is the only Qur'ānic citation.

lii As a verb of piling up, *ḥabā* is heard in a verse of Ru'ba's quoted in *Lisān* art. √*ḥbā*. This verse comes from the end of the final poem in Ru'ba's *Dīwān* as edited by Muḥammad b. Ḥabīb (d. 246/860). To those unfamiliar with the cosmetic gum-darkening once practiced by Arab women of the desert, the last line will ring strangely, but it is a standard of early poetry. Mounded sands as a simile for the curves of a deep-girdled woman's body are nothing new either. What rescues these verses from cliché is the way the desert landscape takes on Salmā's physical attributes, and not the other way around—bespeaking the obsession which is the poem's true theme (lines 23–28 of a 28-line *rajaz* poem):

> Her gentle features are on display, her face uncovered,
> and, covered head to toe in gauzy, threadbare wrappers,
> like **mounds that form** in the scrub of al-Gharīf
> her body shows, tall as the reins of the trim and graceful
> [horse I'm riding]. This stretch of sand is hard on the rear-end rider.
> It sets the darkness of her gums against the shine of bright enamel.
>
> —*Der Dīwān des Reğezdichters Rūba*, 102.

liii *Ḥabiyy* occurs in two separate lightning-scenes of Imru' al-Qays, both in close connection with the "flicker" of lightning called *al-wamīḍ*. In one (*Dīwān Imri' al-Qays* II.458–63), the *wamīḍ* flashes out of mountainous white clouds, from which its light falls upon the *ḥabiyy* (meter: *ṭawīl*):

> "Help me bear the lightning that I see in alps of white,
> whose **flicker** lights [another] **mounded form**.
> Sometimes it stills, and then its glare resurges
> like the arrhythmic stumble of a camel with a broken foot.
> And from the mound there shoot fluorescent streaks
> like the hands of a gambler taking the prize!"
> With my friends I sat waiting on it, somewhere between Ḍārij
> and the emptying of Yathlath's arroyo onto 'Arīḍ.
> Al-Quṭayyāt was hit, and its sandy folds ran over,
> and the wadi of al-Badiyy reached as far as al-Barīḍ.

It swelled the gentle runnels running through low
lush-lands being served with freshwater lashings.
Wide and welcoming are the territories [of which I speak],
their expanses made broad spillways for the rain.
The cloud flushed out its every water-portal.
Lizards fled their homes on the white plains—
May it serve my sister Ḍaʿīfa in her far-off abode:
too far for a visit, except though poetic contrivance.

Then, in his *Muʿallaqa*, the *ḥabiyy* supports a crown of clouds (meter: *ṭawīl*):

> "Companion, do you see the lightning whose *wamīḍ* I am showing you,
> like fluorescent hands [at play] in the crowned *ḥabiyy*?
> The lightning's glare gives light—or are those lamps belonging to a monk
> who causes oil to ride the twisted wicks?"

These verses were quoted on page x of the Introduction. Discerning readers who compare that lightning-scene with the others assembled here might see it as a successful attempt to outdo every other iteration of the motif. The hyperbolic violence of its storm is one sign of this; another is its proliferation of place-names spanning the Arabian Peninsula for hundreds of kilometers. This would suggest that, rather than standing at the beginning of Arabic poetic tradition, Imru' al-Qays's *Muʿallaqa* (or at least its closing section) dates more truly to a later period.

liv To be wrapped in clouds is as normal for the divinity of Judeo-Christian literature (Psalm 18:11–14, Revelations 1:7, *Paradise Lost* I.263–68) as it is for any Near Eastern storm god. The Qur'ān is more circumspect about this, seeming almost to ridicule the notion at *Sūrat al-Baqara* (The Cow) 2:210:

> Do they wait for God to come to them with angels in the shadow of white clouds? In that case, the matter would be settled. All matters go back to God.

God has a seat (*al-kursī*), and according to *Sūrat al-Baqara* 2:255 it is coterminous with the heavens and the earth. He also has a throne (*al-ʿarsh*), and *Sūrat Hūd* 11:7 says it was "above the water" (*ʿalā l-māʾi*) during His creation of the heavens and the earth. So where did God sit before the heavens, earth, and water were there? In answer to this question, raised by an inquisitive Bedouin named Abū Razīn al-ʿUqaylī, the Prophet responded: "He was in **a blind of cloud**, with a void below it and a void above" (*Kāna fī ʿamāʾin taḥtahu hawāʾun wa-fawqahu hawāʾun*). *Musnad al-Imām Aḥmad b. Ḥanbal* XXVI.108.

That is how I might translate the hadith, except for Abū ʿUbayd's statement in *Gharīb al-ḥadith* (Uncommon Vocabulary of Prophetic Narration) II.229: "Only God knows the size and scale of this *ʿamāʾ* and what it was like. But the *ʿamā* that is 'blindness' has nothing to do with the meaning of the hadith." Abū Manṣūr al-Azharī (d. 370/981) cites minority opinion to the contrary in *Tadhīb al-lugha* (The Rectification of Lexicography) III.246, without endorsing it: "I am told that Abū l-Haytham (al-Rāzī, d. 276/889)—in whom I place no great confidence—narrated the hadith with *ʿamā* 'an obscurity,' saying: 'God's location is *ʿamā* because it is beyond description or conception of the descendants of Adam. Everything that is unreachable through mortal intellect is *ʿamā*.'"

lv To say just a few words about Kuthayyir ʿAzza (d. 105/723) is not easy. In his biography, myth and legend combine with dense chapters on Umayyad doxography and statecraft, and other entanglements of a poetic intriguer's life. His life was spent in and around Medina at a time when the empire's seat had left Arabia for Damascus. Although a partisan of the ʿAlid movement, he became a supporter of the Umayyad Caliphate against the Meccan-based revolt of ʿAbd Allāh b. al-Zubayr (d. 73/692), after the latter's imprisonment of Muḥammad b. al-Ḥanafiyya in 66/685. This Muḥammad was a son of ʿAlī b. Abī Ṭālib, and the spiritual head of the sect called al-Kaysāniyya to which Kuthayyir belonged.

Kuthayyir the political poet is still remembered. More often his name is associated with the tenderhearted pioneers of *ghazal* poetry known as the ʿUdhrī school. The pattern of the group was set by Jamīl b. Maʿmar al-ʿUdhrī (d. 65/684-5 or 82/701), whose rhapsode Kuthayyir was, and whose adopted name of *Jamīl Buthayna* "Buthayna's Jamil" identified the poet as his beloved's possession. The pattern's limit-case was personified by "Laylā's Madman": *Majnūn Laylā*, the fictional *poète maudit* to whom a raft of Arabic verse was ascribed in the eighth and ninth centuries CE.

The virtues of the ʿUdhrī school were nonmartial virtues. Its heroism consisted in refusal to renounce desire for an inaccessible beloved, nor to transfer that desire to any other. The ʿUdhrī poets' milieu was remote from cities and their corrupting luxuries, and all of this ill describes Kuthayyir, who was more of an urban eccentric than a desert wanderer. So his career as *Kuthayyir ʿAzza* "ʿAzza's Kuthayyir" requires some explanation.

The judgment of Ṭāhā Ḥusayn (1973), II.295, was that Kuthayyir's infatuation was a calculated pose: "In the Ḥijāz of his day, it was the fashion for poets to bemoan their love for some fair lady; seeing this, Kuthayyir needed a fair lady of his own, and so he began to mention 'Azza in his poems." And Kuthayyir's early critics made the same accusation (*Aghānī* IX.25).

Sincerely put on or not, his 'Udhrī guise vaulted the "real" Kuthayyir out of Umayyad history and into the global pantheon of famous lovers. In at least one version of the *Laylā and Majnūn* saga (that of Jāmī, d. 898/1492), he features as a character. And in Ibn Qutaybā's *Poetry and Poets*, Kuthayyir is shown contributing to the fabric of the Majnūn legend.

We find this in a tale told to the Umayyad caliph 'Abd al-Malik b. Marwān (r. 65–86/685–705), at whose court Kuthayyir was a frequent guest. It is an example of the entertaining *asmār* "night-chats" that took place between poets and caliphs, and it begins with the caliph's question: "Have you ever seen a man more lovesick than yourself? Answer me truthfully."

"Yes, Commander of the Faithful," said Kuthayyir, "yes I have:"

> On my travels through the wasteland, I came upon a man who had set a trap. "What keeps you sitting all the way out here?" I asked him.
>
> "My family and I are starving," he said. "To catch what might relieve us in our hour of need, I set this trap."
>
> I asked him, "If the trap is sprung while I wait here with you, can you see your way to sharing a piece of game with me?"
>
> "Yes," he said. And soon there fell into his trap a doe gazelle. I hurried with him to the trap, but he got there first, and released the doe from the trap and set her free. I said, "What made you do that?"
>
> "I was overcome by tenderness for her resemblance to Laylā!" he said, and extemporized these verses (meter: *ṭawīl*):
>
> "Fear not, dear likeness of Laylā! Today,
> for her sake, I am the beast's friend."
> So I said when I freed the doe from her fetter, and:
> "If you're capable of thanks, then thank Layla!"
> —*Shiʿr* I.416–17; *Dīwān Majnūn Laylā*, 162.

The freeing of the gazelle became a dependable motif in the later Majnūn tradition of Persian narrative poetry. In the *Laylā and Majnūn* by Niẓāmī Ganjawī (d. early seventh/ thirteenth century) it happens twice.

lvi The only other place Kuthayyir's verse reads this way is *K. al-Azmina*, 331, by al-Marzūqī who quotes the *Book of Rain*. In the same author's *Amālī* (Dictations), 364, it is found in the majority reading:

> ... like one who strives to reach the shade of *al-ghamāma*
> to rest beneath, and gets there just when it dissipates.

The poem that it comes from starts like this:

> This, my two companions, is the spot where ʿAzza stayed.
> Tie up your camels, and weep where she passed by.
> Here it is that you can touch the earth that touched her skin.
> The tent that housed her, and the shade that shaded, were both here.
> And if you say your prayers in the place where ʿAzza prayed,
> then God will scrape your record clean of sin.
> Misery and heartache were once unknown to me,
> but here she came, and then there came the time she turned away.
> Is it not the way of women to give and then withhold,
> and make men hate them, like unjust ʿAzza?

There follow thirty-five verses of uninterrupted complaint, which I hate to omit. But the opening verses suffice as context for the last three, which include the verse quoted by Abū Zayd. The words run differently in the poet's *dīwān*—even the word for "cloud" is altered—but their meaning is the same, as the disappointed lover is left to contemplate his parched existence:

> Having gone through her letting go of what was between us,
> I, for all I suffer on account of ʿAzza, am
> like one who strives to reach the shadow of a cloud
> to rest beneath, and gets there just when it dissipates.
> As if the drought-struck land were I, and she were the rain
> holding back until the cloud has traveled on.
> —*Dīwān Kuthayyir ʿAzza*, 95–103; Ibn Jinnī, *al-Khaṣāʾiṣ* I.340.

lvii To call a cloud *al-ʿayn* is to call it a fountain. *Al-ʿayn* is also a "spring," and just about any opening in the earth from which water can be drawn. It is furthermore the Arabic word for "eye." The meaning-bridge of *well* and *eye* is duplicated in Hebrew *ayin*, and turns up in unrelated languages. For discussion of Spanish *ojo de agua* "eye of water," and whether it springs from Arabic *ʿayn*, see Coşeriu (1961), 30–45, who thinks not. In any case, the likeness of terrestrial waters and eyes obtains whether or not it is pre-inscribed in language. Thus Novalis: *Die Ströme sind die Augen einer Landschaft* "The eyes of a landscape are its streams" (*Gesammelte Werke*, 252).

lviii In this one by ʿAdiyy b. al-Riqāʿ (d. after 96/715), it is not a cloud that does the glowering, but a peak of Syria's Anti-Lebanon range called al-Jabal al-Sharqī "The Eastern Mountain." These verses (7–28 of a 28-verse poem) were highlighted by Hibat Allāh ibn al-Shajarī (d. 542/1148) as the best description of lightning in all of Arabic poetry (meter: *basīṭ*):

I wonder at the stillness of my companion of the road,
 the one I roused from sleep, no middling trifler
but a worthy traveler, cradled by the earth
 where slumber felled him, on sloping ground beneath
the hillside's top. Some people turn their outerwear
 to inner when it frays, but not this traveler.
Like one delighting in the drunkard's winy
 cure, or by an apoplexy thrown,
my fellow lay there, and I stood [him up] and told him of the rain
 I could not see, and the lightning [that I could],
sleepless as I was for apprehension: "On the move,
 the crownèd clouds do thunder out their praises.
The North Wind carries water, and dear Mt. Sharqī
 glowers over parties taking shelter in its folds."
The night was expectant, until one who scanned it said:
 "The rain is either hitting al-Ruwayshid or Kharjāʾ."
Awash with blood the view to the west was,
 horizons red with the sun's blotting,
when Dhāt Aḥfār came underneath the bulk of it,
 and lights blared out and vanished into tinsel—

reiterative flame, its newness never dulled
by repetition. Sometimes it causes timber to ignite.
It was during the asterism of al-Jawzāʾ, when pastures
fill with mud, that the cloud settled in for a milking.
Its first release of liquid wore it out, and it lurched on,
weeping at its own exhaustion.
But every wadi's bed that drank its runoff
ran erratically full. Dark and white-capped,
on they ran. Even the wide ones leapt
with spray, and their bends were roiled with churning.
High-water marks were approached, and then they were reached,
and then they were surpassed, and the wadis ran over.
Calling to itself the flow pushed downward by the
hills, the sandy bottom gaped and jabbered.
The narrow branches of the ancient watercourse
were all made wadis, hauling crystal waters
between clean pebbled margins. Any greenery
they contain is clear at the wadi bottom.
Its outthrown boulders form dense masses, harder
than an axe's blade. And all day long, stuck
high upon a busted trunk of tree, and waiting it out
with elbows splayed, the chameleon hangs on,
like a poor old man whose robe's been yanked away,
with no more care for appearances, and bare knuckles.

—*Al-Ḥamāsa al-Shajariyya* II.783; *Dīwān shiʿr ʿAdiyy b. al-Riqāʿ*, 145–49.

lix In these verses by Ru'ba's father al-ʿAjjāj, *al-ʿayn* has its own *qibla*. In praise of a chieftain of Quraysh, he said (lines 47–50 of a 180-line *rajaz* poem):

To behold him is like gazing out at
the night. When roused to anger, he rumbles like
a nocturnal storm **from the direction of *al-ʿayn***, as it drives on
the rearing clouds and springtime's major rains.

—*Dīwān al-ʿAjjāj*, 18–19.

On the strength of this and other literary evidence, William Sersen deduces that prayers for rain were directed southwest from Iraq before Islam. "This direction was thought not to fail to bring rain—hence, the statement 'we have had rain by *al-ʿayn*,' with its inherent concept of *fiʿl* ['effective agency']—, and may originally have been associated with the sacrifice of cattle, at least in a certain quarter, or quarters.... It is important to question why any particular direction should have been considered as propitious for rain, let alone become the object of an *istimṭār* ceremony. As noted previously, there are frequent references in the *kutub al-anwāʾ* to the south wind as characteristically driving on the rain clouds. This would, in part, suggest an actual phenomenological basis for *al-ʿayn*." Sersen (1976), 82.

On the subject of pre-Islamic prayer for rain, the best-known Arabic account is by al-Jāḥiẓ, whose unnamed source is Hishām b. al-Kalbī (d. 204 or 206/819 or 821). It will remind some of a scene in Livy (*Ab urbe condita* XXII.16–17):

> In time of severe drought, the early pagan Arabs used fire to beg for for rain. If the ordeal went on without abating, and they were obliged to resort to rain-supplication, they would get together and round up as many cattle as they could. To their tails and between their hamstrings, they lashed sticks of *salaʿ* and *ʿushar*, and then drove them up to the mountain wastes, where they set fire to them, raising a din with their prayers and entreaties. Their belief was that rain would be induced by this procedure. This is what the poem by Umayya (b. Abī l-Ṣalt, early seventh century) is about (meter: *khafīf*):
>
> Out in the thorn-trees, the folk you see, they of the droning clamor,
> have suffered visitation by a year of biting drought.
> They who, in times gone by, would not eat
> unleavened things now gobble dry flour.
> Out of the flatlands and up the mountain's side they drive
> emaciated cattle, harrying them with fear of their demise,
> with burning torches tight in the short hairs of their tails,
> tied there so that "seas" be stirred [out of the skies],
> until they are roasted through, and a cloud rears up above them,
> and another upward-rearing cloud is driven to its side,
> and the Divinity sees it mark [the earth] with precipitation
> when a rain-bringing South Wind finally blows for them.

The lofty cloud pours down its water, a rain to put
an end to calamity, now averted
by a quantity of *salaʿ* and *ʿushar*-wood to match it,
no easy burden for the cattle freighted by it.
—*Ḥayawān* IV.466–67, cited by Sersen (1976), 78–79.

lx Terrestrial waters are where travel halts for animals and people alike. In a poem by Dhū l-Rumma, a roving herd of onagers is greeted by the rising sun's reflection in the *jadāwil* of a deserted oasis (verses 41–49 of a 71-verse poem, meter: *ṭawīl*):

The light of morning finally broke over
rivulets that gleamed like cutting swords.
When they arrived and found the waters
unattended, it was no time for sleepy eyes to rest.
They went around and searched it from all angles.
All pathways to the water bobbed with their tails.
Their wariness dispelled, they arranged themselves cheek to cheek
at the water's brimming edge, to the frogs' clamor,
stirring the water's coldness and bringing down its level.
Despite their fear, they entered the running stream up to their knees.
To remedy their burning insides, their gulps
were [heaving] like sand-grouse breasts.
While all were drinking, and none left craving
the shimmering remedy for thirst, they remained on guard,
straining their ears for the twang of a bow driving
the nock of a fine-feathered arrow at the target
of a hidden hunter. They listen for his rustle,
and the taut report of what pins victims to the spot.
—*Dīwān Dhī l-Rumma* II.804–8.

lxi *Lisān* art. √*qnā* gives the opinion that *qanāt* is the singular form, *qanā* the plural, and *quniyy* the plural of the plural.

lxii As a catchment whose water becomes drinkable as it settles, *al-kurr* (pl. *al-kirār*) is attested in *Lisān* art. √*krr* by these verses of Kuthayyir which (as is often the case) appear differently in Kuthayyir's *dīwān* (meter: *ṭawīl*):

My love for you will last as long as *washīja*
grows in the Najd, and Mt. Ublā and Mt. Tiʿār
stand firm—as long as mirages frolic [in the desert],
and there run stampedes of white-footed game,
and ʿĀdite wells and **holding pools**
are sweetened by Tihāma's wadi and its flow,
watered in the season of al-Jawzāʾ and the Bucket
by ephebic clouds of white, their teats unbound
and streaming to the Najd, where stone hollows
beneath the ground of Najd await their cutting loose.
—*Dīwān Kuthayyir ʿAzza*, 427.

There is also, according to *Lisān*, a quantitative side to *al-kurr*, naming the minimum amount of groundwater that must accumulate for it to be considered pollution-free.

lxiii *Al-ʿudmul* is water whose long standing has left it pure and drinkable. *Lisān* art. √*ʿdml* illustrates it with a verse by Labīd b. Rabīʿa (meter: *ṭawīl*):

The women trek for water from Ghawl's abundant supply,
and **well-aged waters** from Manʿij of the blue surfaces.
—*Sharḥ Dīwān Labīd*, 241.

Labīd (d. ca. 40/660) was half-brother to the same Arbad b. Qays mentioned above in note l, and is credited with ten separate elegies for him. In this one, Arbad's death by lightning is clearly referenced (meter: *basīṭ*):

Death leaves no one bare [of its shroud],
caring nothing for worries of parent or child.
The disasters I dreaded for Arbad were many.
Little did I fear the stars that hit him,
nor the hateful day's thunder, nor the bolts that took away
my tireless, heroic horseman,

the warrior who redressed the victims of war,
giving once, and then twice to the two-time suppliant.
Beyond whatever was asked for, he rained
like a greenery-raising burst of springtime.
[And now,] on the night that wholes are made fragments,
my eye meets nothing it wants to rest on.
It is the way of freeborn sons
to wind up poor, plenty though they be in number.
If they attract envy, so do they attract death,
and all their earthly power ends in ruin.
When have you not wept for Arbad, my eye?
When the foe stood, and we stood there in horror?
When else have you not wept for Arbad, my eye?
When lopped branches are stirred by winter winds
gravid [with war] and dry of goodness,
blowing away the remnants of our tribe?
Impassive while others ran senseless was Arbad,
and when they showed purpose, so much more did he,
who was noble and sweet, yet bitter in sweetness.
In essence, a graceful man down to his core
has driven his mourners to grievous distraction,
like deer with green horns left to wander the plains.

—*Sharḥ Dīwān Labīd*, 158–62, with considerable variation in *al-Sīra al-nabawiyya* (The Life of the Prophet) IV.569–70 of Ibn Isḥāq (d. ca. 151/768) and Ibn Hishām (d. 219/833).

lxiv Renaud (1947), 45.

lxv *Ḍaḥḍāḥ* and *ḍaḥl* are both heard in this rain-description by Tamīm b. Muqbil (d. after 37/657) from the middle of a 43-line poem (meter: *ṭawīl*):

Lightning had me sleepless, just before the end of night,
at the edge of Mt. Rammān's stony apron. Black and brilliant
clouds from the north brought it, and every time I said "That's that,"
it erupted, and the green bee-eaters winged away in the flood.

The dawn of al-Simāk's tenure came up over
a noisy log of cloud pouring down Mt. Shurma's skirts.
At midday, the wooded clefts of Mt. Raqd came beneath it.
Its runoff was substantial, no **shallow thing** nor a **surface trifle.**
At Sharj and al-Ṣarīf, the white clouds staggered, overburdened,
then deposited their heavy water-load,
and every wadi ran full of it, [foaming white] as the
ground where itinerant salt-vendors have set up shop.

—*Dīwān Ibn Muqbil*, 42–43.

"Asian green bee-eater" is the common name of *Merops orientalis*, called in Arabic *qāriya*, pl. *qawārī*. In the second of these verses, Hussein (2009), 221–22, understands them to have met their deaths by drowning. To make a hurried departure from the lightning-scene (like the wet-winged rails in Mulayḥ's poem in note xxxii to *al-khafaqān*) is normal bird behavior, though, and my wishful understanding is that the green bee-eaters are inconvenienced by the summer rain but not destroyed by it.

lxvi *Lisān* art. √*hrshm* defines the feminine noun *hirshamma* as "a copious milker," when said of goats and camels, and this is nothing to puzzle over as milk is an expression for water throughout the *Book of Rain*. In the second line, I read the verb *tabdhulu* as second-person masculine "you give freely," and the well as a metaphor for the patron's generosity, though it might equally be read as third-person feminine "*it* gives freely." In that case, the patron disappears, and a description of the well chiseled through rock is all it is.

Where the line appears two generations later, in *Majālis Thaʿlab* (Seated Gatherings of Abū l-ʿAbbās Thaʿlab), 203, I still take it metaphorically. The lines that follow it are kind of obscure, until you picture the annoyance of having to wait while others dawdle at the well, treating it like a hair salon:

Filled up to your ancient rim,
bored through a hollow of *hirshamm*,
you give freely to neighbors and to cousins,
while others at the well play dumb
and dress their hair like hornless rams.

[lxvii] At *nashifa yanshafu*, (11r11) a marginal note says that Abū Ḥātim held *nashafa yanshifu* to be the correct voweling.

[lxviii] Bräunlich (1926), 9. This kind of aquifer is no doubt what Kuthayyir meant by "stone hollows" (*ghiwār*) in the verse at note lxii. In a verse by Imru' al-Qays in praise of his horse, it is the figure of a self-regenerating resource:

> After his exertions, he recovers his forces on the go,
> the way a *ḥisy* fills back up after its portals are churned [by buckets].
> —*Dīwān Imri' al-Qays* II.468. (This is verse 17 from the same poem quoted above in note liii to *al-ḥabiyy*.)

[lxix] Cheikho (17n1) notes that *aḍa'a*, written with a second *hamza* in manuscript (fol. 11v2), appears in all lexica as *aḍāt*, with initial hamza only.

[lxx] An oasis called Falja, said to lie on the road from Mecca to Basra, is memorialized in an anonymous pair of verses:

> How I love the hills of Falja in the morning,
> and the canopies pitched up their sides.
> They say that Falja's waters are funny-tasting brine,
> and so they are. But to the heart, they're sweet.
> —Ibn Khallikān, *Wafayāt al-aʿyān* (The Deaths of Eminent Men) V.320 (art. Yazīd b. al-Ṭathriyya).

[lxxi] Meissner (1896), 185–86. The Pallukkatu canal's location is not precisely known; some geological grounds for excluding Falluja itself as its branching-site are summarized by Boiy and Verhoeven (1998), 154–55.

[lxxii] In *Sūrat Maryam* (Mary) 19:86, ***wird*** is used of a party of sinners on their way to Hell:

> We will drive the grave offenders to Gehenna **in a thirsty mob**.

[lxxiii] The plural of *ṭuḥlub* is *ṭaḥālib*. This word occurs at the end of Dhū l-Rumma's description of a cobweb-choked well, cited just ahead in note lxxvi to *al-kawkab* (where it is translated as "greeny scum").

[lxxiv] *Asina l-rajul* is my emendation of *Asina l-mā'* "The **water** became altered for the

worse" (thus in manuscript at fol. 12r11). *Asina l-māʾ* is correct usage, but it strays from the point being made about *asan* as a word for "fainting" and its alternation with *wasn* in Kilābī dialect. This emendation has the backing of *Lisān* art. √*ʾsn*: "*Asina l-rajul* 'The man fainted,' verbal noun *asan*," and Abū Zayd's own *K. al-Hamz* (The Book of *Hamza*), 30:

> *Asina l-māʾ* is said when water undergoes a change for the worse. [In the imperfect tense, the verb may be voweled as] *yaʾsanu or yaʾsunu*, verbal noun *asan*. ***Asina l-rajul* is said when a man is overcome by noxious fumes**, sometimes to the point of death, [and in this sense its imperfect tense is voweled exclusively as] *yaʾsanu*. A poet said:
>
> *at-tāriku l-qirana muṣfarran anāmiluhu*
> *yamīlu fī r-rumḥi mayla l-māʾiḥi l-**asini***
>
> ... leaving the foe limp and yellow, like someone **overcome**
> **by the fumes** of a well, and their fingers lose their grip around their spears.

The verse is by Zuhayr b. Abī Sulmā (d. early seventh century CE), in praise of his patron Harim b. Sinān, with slight variations in Zuhayr's *Dīwān* as edited by Thaʿlab (meter: *basīṭ*):

> Don't you know how well showered with acclaim
> Ibn Sinān is, and how much he lays out for that acclaim?
> And how distinguished for self-control he is in every house
> of the kind that cowards and penny-pinchers shun?
> When you see his fighters and their surly horses
> charging, and their shields and swords of Indian make,
> up to the encounter where blow follows blow
> the way that trunks of palm are chopped with axes,
> the foe goes limp and yellow, like someone **overcome**
> **by the fumes** of a well, and their fingers lose their grip around their spears.
>
> —*Sharḥ shiʿr Zuhayr b. Abī Sulmā*, 98–99.

What was the dizzying agent in the wells? Carbon dioxide, maybe, or some other fume expelled by Arabia's mineral deposits.

lxxv "Ground-breaking," in English, is the work of the plow. By contrast, a remark attributed to the caliph ʿUmar b. al-Khaṭṭāb (d. 23/644) uses the well-digger's work as a metaphor for artistic innovation: "Imruʾ al-Qays has preeminence. It was he who **broke through rock to dig the well** of the fountain of poetry for them" (***khasafa*** *la-hum ʿayn al-shiʿr*). *Shiʿr* I.68, *Aghānī* VIII.142.

lxxvi *Al-kawkab* is also said for "the greater part" of any large mass, such as an army, an expanse of grazing-land, or a body of water. In this sense, there is nothing necessarily brilliant about *al-kawkab*—least of all in Dhū l-Rumma's description of a decrepit watering-hole (meter: *ṭawīl*):

How many gift robes have I held up like pennants [to block the sun],
on days that locusts' feet hop, blistered where they tread the stone?
How many [spiders'] houses have I torn the roofs of, sinking
down to a *kawkab* that makes its drinker's face recoil,
with [a water-bag] fastened to a strap from my own saddle, inching
quickly to the water where it parts the greeny scum?
—*Dīwān Dhī l-Rumma* II.852–53.

lxxvii *Qarīḫa* has a cognate in the Hebrew verb *karah* "to dig," heard in the very ancient "Song of the Well" of Numbers 21:17–18.

In Arabic, *al-qarīḫa* is heard in a verse by Ibn Harma al-Qurashī (ca. 176/792), bemoaning the outcome of a love affair (meter: *wāfir*):

You're like **the first flow of a well**, sweet
when tapped, that later on runs briny.
—*Shiʿr Ibn Harma al-Qurashī*, 79.

lxxviii *Ghibāʾ* is unvoweled in manuscript (12v12), and could be read as *ghabāʾ* (thus Cheikho). However, *Lisān* art. √*ghbā* defines *al-ghabāʾ* as a synonym of *al-ghubār* "The Dust Cloud," and *al-ghibāʾ* as dirt cast over a well in order to conceal it. While their common root, √*ghbā*, connects both words to "stupidity" (*al-ghabāwa*), their meanings also suggest a link to √*ghbn*, which is a root for deception and concealment.

lxxix *Ranaq* is heard in an ascetic sermon of ʿAlī b. Abī Ṭālib: "The world's claim is weak, her drink **murky**, and the path to her waterhole thick with mud." Al-Qāḍī al-Quḍāʿī (d. 454/1062), *A Treasury of Virtues*, tr. Qutbuddin, 65.

lxxx The early Nabataean communities of Northwest Arabia spoke Aramaic alongside the dialect that later evolved into the Arabic language. The bilingual Nabataean inscription of ʿEn ʿAvdat, dating to the first century BCE or CE, is the earliest Arabic-language inscription known.

The polities of the Nabataeans collapsed in the third century CE with the failure of long-distance trade, beginning a period of economic decline in the Arabian Peninsula that persisted up to the seventh century. Later on, in the Islamic period, the ethnonyms *Nabaṭ*, *Nabīṭ*, and *Nabāṭī* (pl. *Anbāṭ*) were applied to Christian communities in Syria and Iraq that retained their Aramaic dialects. As such, it was a despective label, connoting village squalor and a poor command of the Arabic language. (Al-Aṣmaʿī's low opinion of the poet al-Kumayt, cited above in note xiii to *al-ḥafsha*, is an example of this prejudice.) With the change in this ethnonym's application came a change in its imagined derivation: *Lisān* art. √*nbṭ* says nothing of well-digging where the Anbāṭ of Syria and Iraq are concerned, but says they were so called for their lives of agrarian labor spent "**coaxing out** the produce of their lands" (*li-**stinbāṭihim** mā yakhruju min al-arḍayn*).

lxxxi *Ujāj* is heard in the Qurʾān at *Sūrat al-Wāqiʿa* (The Event) 56:70, quoted above in note xxxvi to *al-muzn*. It also occurs in *Sūrat al-Furqān* (The Criterion) 25:53 along with three other water-epithets mentioned in this passage, and in the same order:

> It is He that drives two seas alongside, one *ʿadhbun furātun* "drinkable and sweet," the other *milḥun ujājun* "caustic brine," and He enforces their separation with a barrier in between.

Freshwater sources in the sea are found all over the world, and were known to Mediterranean seafarers in ancient times. Strabo (d. ca. 21 CE) notes one such discharge site off the coast of Syria, from which the islanders of Arados (modern Arwād) drew fresh water through leather hoses (*Geography* XVI.2.13).

lxxxii *Al-imiddān* is heard in this *ṭawīl*-meter verse complaining of old age:

> Now it happens that women avoid my company, the way
> gazelles avoid a cistern full of **hypersaline** water.

Lisān art. √*mdd* attributes it to Zayd al-Khayl or Abū l-Ṭamaḥān al-Qaynī (cf. art. √*qhā*), two poets who were active during the Prophet's lifetime and made mid-career conversions to Islam.

lxxxiii The manuscript (14r8) has *al-ḥamaʾa*, which Gottheil retains but Cheikho emends correctly to *al-ḥam'a*—thus voweled in *Nawādir al-lugha*, 353, and Ibn al-Aʿrābī's *K. al-Bi'r*, 57, where the pre-Islamic poet Ḥātim al-Ṭā'ī praises the generosity of his hosts (meter: *kāmil*):

In an evil hour, I sought their protection—such an excellent
tribe, in hard times and easy ones.
I was served life-giving water, not
left to pound *ham'a* [at the bottom] of a dig.

lxxxiv On *al-ghiryan*, *Lisān* art. √*ghrn* quotes al-Aṣmaʿī: "When flowing water covers the earth and then dries up, *al-ghiryan* is the layer of fissured clay seen coating the earth's surface, as heard in the *rajaz* verses:

Like the cracking of **dried clay** is the cracking
of her wrinkles, when she [smiles as she] draws near me.

APPENDIX

ON THE NAMES OF THE WIND

by Abū ʿAbd Allāh al-Ḥusayn b. Aḥmad b. Khālawayh
(d. 371/980-81)

Arabic is so rich in words for winds and breezes, and so few are mentioned in the *Book of Rain*, that one might suspect Abū Zayd of reserving the subject for another book. But no Book of Winds is attributed to him by anyone. I append therefore this text as a coda.

As shown in the transmission statement of the *Book of Trees and Herbage*, Ibn Khālawayh belonged to the fourth generation of scholars after Abū Zayd. Readers of his *Names of the Lion* will find him more loquacious in *On the names of the wind*, which begins with an exegesis of *rīḥ* "wind" before listing its names and epithets. The text was authored by Ibn Khālawayh in the familiar sense that he composed and published it as a written document, as opposed to the orally-delivered lecture that was Abū Zayd's medium. It seems to be Ibn Khālawayh's expansion on the list of names for wind that he gives in *Sharḥ al-Maqṣūra*, 311–12, being his commentary on the didactic poem *al-Maqṣūra* by Ibn Durayd, who was one of his teachers. (The whole of this poem is copied on folios 61r–89r of Bnf MS 4231 Arabe, the same seventh/thirteenth-century codex that holds the *Book of Rain*.)

One late-sixteenth-century manuscript of *On the names of the wind* has been edited twice, by Ignaz Kratchkovsky in 1926 and Ḥātim Ṣāliḥ al-Ḍāmin in 1974. This manuscript (St. Petersburg State University MS O 839) is of special interest for the hand that copied it, that of Madyan b. ʿAbd al-Raḥmān al-Qūṣūnī (d. after 1044/1634) who later became head of the famous Manṣūrī hospital complex on al-Muʿizz Street in Cairo. His original writings include *Qāmūs al-aṭibbāʾ wa-nāmūs al-alibbāʾ* (The Dictionary for Doctors and Natural Law for the Perspicacious), a work dated to 1038/1628, some twenty-five years after he copied out Ibn Khālawayh's treatise.

This manuscript is marred by a missing leaf between folios 29 and 30. Its contents are restored from a second manuscript held in Cairo (Dār al-Kutub MS 5252 ه), which was edited by Ḥusayn Muḥammad Muḥammad Sharaf and published at Medina under the title *al-Rīḥ* (The Wind) in 1984.

♦

In the name of God, the Merciful, the Compassionate.

The grammarian Abū ʿAbd Allāh al-Ḥusayn ibn Khālawayh said: Praise be to God, Lord of the two worlds, and God's blessings and peace be upon our master Muḥammad, and all his relations and companions.

Al-rīḥ, the word for "wind," is a feminine noun; its diminutive is *ruwayḥa*. God, be He exalted and magnified, says [that unjust dealings blight the world] "like a wind with frost in it."[1] *Ṣirr*, the word for "frost," is also heard in the hadith: "There is no harm in eating the locust killed by *al-ṣirr*."[2]

God, be He exalted and magnified, says: "When you are sped in ships by a kindly wind . . ."[3] [Here, *rīḥ* is modified by a feminine adjective, but in the same verse] God mentions "a wind that is violent" [where *rīḥ* is modified by a masculine participle]. There are two ways of explaining this. One is by comparison to the way that [masculine participles] *ḥāʾiḍ* "expelling blood" and *ṭāmith* "menstruant" are applied to women during their monthly period. Alternately, it is said to be [a truncation of the genitive phrase] "a wind of violence." As for *al-rīḥ al-ʿaqīm* "the unfruitful wind," the adjective is feminine even though it lacks the feminine suffix.[4] This is because of traditional Arab usage, in which the masculine adjective *ʿaqīm* "barren" is applied to women and men equally. Wind that is *ʿaqīm* communicates no fecundating power to the trees.

A favorable turn of fortune may be called a "wind," where the Blessed and Almighty says: "lest your wind cease"—that is, "the opportunity We gave you to prevail over them."[5]

Rīḥ was at one time pronounced **riwḥ*, before the medial *wāw* disappeared through vocalic shift. Its plural is *arwāḥ*, on the pattern of *aḥwāḍ*, the plural of *ḥawḍ* "pool," and it occurs in these verses recited to us by Ibn Durayd (meter: *wāfir*):

A tent that admits the flutter of winds
  is dearer to me than the lofty castle,
and my solace in donning a woolen cloak
  is dearer to me than the gauzy wrapper[6].

The plural **aryāḥ*, adduced by al-Liḥyānī in his *Nawādir* (Lexical Rarities), is spurious.[7] As for *rīḥān*, Ibn Mujāhid (d. 324/936) told me on the authority of al-Simmarī (d. 277/890) that al-Farrā' (d. 207/822) said: "*Rīḥān* is the plural of *rūḥ* 'spirit' in the way that *kīzān* is the plural of *kūz* 'cup,' or *nīnān* of *nūn* 'whale.'"

Wind is what brings down the various rains—*al-qaṭr*, *al-wadq*, *al-ghayth*—to which God, be He exalted and magnified, refers collectively as *al-raḥma* "mercy," saying: "It is He who sends the winds as glad tidings in advance of His *raḥma*," that is, in advance of the rain.[8]

Wind and rain combine to bring down *al-ghayth*, dispelling barrenness and drought, and reviving fecundity and growth. Fertility and growth are signs of God's approval of His worshippers' actions, blessed and exalted be He—or have you not heard the Almighty's words?

> [Noah said:] "I told them, 'Beg for your Lord's forgiveness, for truly forgiving is He. / He sends the sky above you into torrents, / and **increases** you in herds and offspring, and forms gardens for you, and rivers.'"[9]

Ibn Khālawayh said: Here, [IVth-form verb] *amdada* is used for "increase" of what is good; for increase of what is bad [IInd-form] *maddada* is used, as where God the Blessed and Almighty says: "He **increases** them in straying and dissipation."[10]

The Arabs say: "When *al-mu'tafikāt* 'The Inverters' are many, the lands prosper," meaning those winds that lift the topsoil and turn it over.[11] Slander is called *al-ifk* because it is an "inversion" of the truth.

Al-nas͟hāṣ is the cloud that comes from the direction of *al-ʿayn*, which is the direction of the *qibla*.[12] When the South Wind fecundates it, the North Wind sets it flowing, and the East Wind hastens its ripening, this is the most abundant source of rain there is.

Ummāt al-riyāḥ "The Mothers of the Winds" are four.[13] The plural word for human mothers is *ummahāt*, but in this expression, *ummāt*—the plural for mother cows—is used. The North Wind, *al-Shamāl*, brings Arabia refreshing breezes. The South Wind, *al-Janūb*, brings rain, mist, humidity, and the soaking dew called *al-g͟hamaq*. The East Wind, *al-Ṣabā*, is what fecundates the trees.

When two lovers come together it is said that their wind is a South Wind, as in the anonymous verse (meter: *ṭawīl*):

> Should the wind of our love become a North Wind, then by my life
> I'll turn anew [my steps toward you] when it blows again from the South.

When lovers separate, their wind is said to be from the North, because the North Wind splits the clouds while the South Wind drives them together. Another poet said (meter: *ṭawīl*):

> The passing East Wind buffets the scrubland lodger,
> but the stirring of the South Wind breaks my heart,
> that South Wind lately come from where my beloved is.
> What soul is safe from passion where the beloved used to stay?[14]

And another:

> O wind, bring me greetings
> from one whose greetings never come.
> Bring it, and tug on the clothes they're wearing,
> that a breeze from my dear one come with you.

The West Wind, *al-Dabūr*, is a tribulation and a hardship from which I seek God's refuge. The slightest West Wind is violent, and brings distress to the eyes. This is why God's Prophet, God's blessings and peace be upon him, used to say at the stirring of the wind, "Please, God, let it be the winds, and not a Wind." Out of all the winds, only the West Wind confers no benefit whatsoever.

Each of the other winds brings some form of good, although Kuthayyir vilified the North Wind and called it *ʿaqīm*, saying (meter: *ṭawīl*):

... barrenly, it kicks up the sifted dust.[15]

Accordingly, Abū ʿAmr b. al-ʿAlāʾ and ʿĀṣim preferred that every doom-bringing wind mentioned in the Qurʾān be read in the singular, and that beneficent winds be read in the plural.[16] And Sībawayhi quotes the verse (meter: *ṭawīl*):

No share of noble lineage has he, nor does
the South Wind or the East blow him any favors.[17]

Where God, be He exalted and magnified, says that He gave Solomon control of the wind, one might ask why it is always in the singular.[18] The answer is that God gave Solomon power over the *Ṣabā* alone: "a fair breeze, which blew as he willed" (38:36) and carried his throne in half a day from Kabul to Qazwīn, which is a journey of one month.

The Prophet, God's blessing and peace be upon him, said: "I was given victory by the East Wind; and by the West Wind was ʿĀd destroyed."[19] And Ibn ʿArafa Nifṭawayh (d. 323/935) recited to me this verse in praise of the Prophet, God's blessings and peace be upon him (meter: *ṭawīl*):

His prayer is answered with a wind from the East
sent by God to prosper corn and *abb*.

This last word, meaning "pasturage," occurs in a verse I heard from Ibn Durayd (meter: *ramal*):

Our line is Qays, the Najd our home
and *abb*, and where we sate our passions.

Where God speaks of the garden "struck by a whirlwind with fire in it, and burnt up," the phrase is explained by Ibn ʿAbbās (d. 68/687) as "the wind that brings the *samūm*."[20] So I was told by Abū ʿAbd Allāh al-Qāḍī [al-Ḥusayn b. Ismāʿīl al-Maḥāmilī, d. 330/941], on the authority of al-Dawraqī (d. 252/866),[21] on the authority of ʿUbayd Allāh al-Ashjaʿī (d. 182/798), who heard it from Hārūn b. ʿAntara (d. 142/759), who transmitted it on the authority of his father. And I was informed by Abū Ḥafṣ b. al-Shaḥḥām (?) on the authority of Abū ʿArūba (d. 318/930), on the authority of al-Ashajj (d. 257/871), on the authority of Ḥafṣ b. Ghayyāth (d. 194/810), on the authority of Dāʾūd b. Abī Hind (d. 140/758), on the authority of ʿIkrima (d. 107/726) that Ibn ʿAbbās said: "The East Wind came to the North Wind and said, 'Come along, that we may bring victory to God's Prophet, God's blessings and peace be upon him.' The North Wind said: 'A noble dame does not travel by night.'[22] So it was the East Wind alone that brought victory to God's Prophet, God's blessings and peace be upon him."

In the hadith: "I feel the wind of your Lord from the direction of Yemen" (*Innī la-ajidu rīḥa rabbikum min qibali l-Yaman*), "Yemen" is a reference to the Anṣār, who defended him and ensured his victory.[23] [Alternately, the hadith is reported as] "I feel the *nafas* 'breath' of your Lord," meaning that the Lord God used the Anṣār to reassure the Prophet of his own survival, and that the Prophet's awareness of this was like a sensory perception.

NAMES OF THE WIND

The North Wind's name has six different forms: *al-shamʾal*, *al-shamāl*, *al-shaʾmal*, *al-shamal*, *al-shaml*, and *al-shamūl*.[24] The South Wind is *al-janūb*, also *al-azyab* "The Sprightly" and *al-jirbiyāʾ* "The Mangy" (?).[25] The East Wind is *al-ṣabā*, also *al-qabūl* "The Faceable." The West Wind is *al-dabūr* "The Unfaceable".[26] Any wind coming from between these points is called *nakbāʾ* "oblique."

[The blowing of the cardinal winds may be expressed as Ist-form verbs:] *Shamalat*, *janabat*, *dabarat*, and *ṣabat* are all said [with *al-rīḥ* as the implied subject of them all]. But [the IVth-form verb] *anʿamat* is said solely in reference to *al-nuʿāmī* "The Benefactory" [variously defined as a Northwest Wind, a South Wind, or a wind that blows southeast].

Al-shaffān "The Cloak Thinner" is a cold wind, and so are *al-balīl* "The Wet and Cold," *al-ṣirr* "The Frost," *al-ḥarjaf* "The Chill," and *al-qirra* "The Cooler."

Al-muʾtafika "The Inverter" [was discussed earlier]. *Maḥwa* "The Effacer" [is mentioned in *rajaz* by al-Qulākh b. Ḥazn]:

Day began with an effacer's ruckus,
which wreaked itself upon the frail of the herd.[27]

Al-rukhāʾ "The Gentle," *al-ruhāʾ* "The Lightfoot," *al-rāḥa* "The Slack," *al-rayda* and *al-raydāna* "The Soft," and *al-munshira* "The Relaxing" (?) [are all words for gentle winds].

Al-mutadhaʾʾiba "The Wolfish" is a wind that blows from all directions. It is so called after the wolf's behavior when it falls silent on one side and then attacks from another. Ibn al-Anbārī (d. 328/940) recited to me (meter: *basīṭ*):

Oppressed by damp, the onager is kept awake
by the **wolfishness** of the wind, its whispers, and hard rains.[28]

Al-kharīq "The Rent Open,"[29] *al-ʿāṣif*, *al-ʿāṣifa*, *al-muʿṣif*, and *al-muʿṣifa* "The Violent," *al-muʿṣir* "The Cyclonic," *al-muʿijja* "The Ruckus-Causer," *al-munsifa* "The Disperser," *al-munshiba* "The Entangler," *al-ṣarṣar* "The Droning Gale,"[30] and *al-hāriya* (?)[31] are all distinctly cold.

Al-nāfija "The Scatter," *al-sayhūk* and *al-sayhūj* "Winds that Turn Solid Ground Into Dust," *al-sākira* "The Inebriate," *al-ḥā'ira* "The Befuddled," and *al-hayf* "The Leaf-Wilter" are all hot, and so are *al-ḥarūr* "The Hot Blast" and *al-samūm* "The Poisonously Hot."[32] Ibn Mujāhid of blessed memory told us on the authority of al-Simmarī that al-Farrā' said: "*Al-ḥarūr* is for the heat of night, and *al-samūm* the heat of day."[33]

'Umar b. al-Fatḥ was a fine fellow. On the authority of Ibn Zanjawayh (d. 251/865), he told me that Hishām [b. 'Ammār, d. 245/859] narrated on the authority of al-Walīd [b. Muslim, d. 195/810] that 'Abd al-Malik b. Jurayḥ (d. 150/767) heard from 'Aṭā' [b. Abī Rabāḥ, d. ca. 114/732] that 'Ā'isha said:[34] "Any time the wind blew up, the Prophet, God's blessings and peace be upon him, used to say: 'For good winds, and the good they bring, dear God, I beg You. And against bad winds, and the bad they bring, be my refuge.'"[35]

'Umar also said: "The jurist Abū 'Abd Allāh b. al-Ḍaḥḥāk informed me that Bundār [Muḥammad b. Bashshār, d. 252/866] informed him on the authority of 'Abd al-Raḥmān b. Mahdī (d. 198/814), on the authority of Sufyān [al-Thawrī, d. 161/778], on the authority of Salama [b. Dīnār al-Makhzūmī, d. ca. 140/757], on the authority of Abū l-Aḥwaṣ ['Awf b. Mālik al-Jushamī, d. before 100/718] that 'Alī b. Abī Ṭālib described *al-sakīna* in the following way. 'It has a face like a human face, and after that it is a fleeting wind.' And according to another account: 'Its face is like the face of a cat.'"[36]

Al-azyab is heard in a hadith of the Prophet, God's blessings and peace be upon him: "In Paradise, God created wind after wind for seven years. Before them stands a closed gate, but the Spirit (*al-Rūḥ*) reaches you from gaps in it. If not for this gate, everything between heaven and earth would be smashed to bits. The wind you call *al-janūb* is called by God *al-azyab*."[37] Sufyān averred that the people of Bahrain use this word for the South Wind too.

The forward part of any wind is called its *'uthnūn* "chin hair." Its rearward quarters are its *adhyāl* "tails," and its upper parts are its *aʿrāf* "crests." I heard Ibn al-Anbārī say: "The singular of *aʿrāf* is *ʿurf*," and he contrasted it with *anfāl* and *ankāl*, whose singular forms follow an altogether different paradigm.[38]

Scholarly opinion differs on *Sūrat al-Ḥijr* (Hegra) 15:22 [where *lawāqiḥ*, seemingly a plural active participle, is heard in apposition to the singular noun *al-rīḥ*]:

> We send the winds as **fecundators**, and send down water from the sky for you to drink. You are not the water's keepers.

Some say that *lawāqiḥ* are winds that "fecundate" (*tulqiḥu*) the trees and seasonal pasturelands. Abū ʿUbayda said: "*Lawāqiḥ* is an allomorph of *malāqiḥ*, the plural of [feminine IVth-form participle] *mulqiḥa*, in which the initial consonant has fallen away." Others object, saying that **mulqiḥa* is never heard, and that [masculine Ist-form participle] *lāqiḥ* is used in its place, much the way *ʿaqīm* is used for the wind in preference to **muʿqima*. Thus did Abū ʿAmr al-Shaybānī explain *lawāqiḥ* as the plural of *lāqiḥ* "fecundating," comparing it to *lābin* "milk-yielding" and *tāmir* "date-bearing."

ʿUmar b. al-Fatḥ reported to me on the authority of Isḥāq b. Ḥabīb, who heard from Abū Ibrāhīm al-Turjumānī (d. 235/848) that ʿUbays [b. Maymūn al-Taymī] heard from Abū l-Muhazzam [Yazīd b. Sufyān]: "I heard the Prophet say, God's blessings and peace be upon him: 'The *rīḥ lawāqiḥ* mentioned in God's book is the South Wind, which blows from Paradise to bring benefits to humankind. And the North Wind blows from Hell, but on its way through Paradise it collides with a breeze that brings its temperature down.'"[39]

Among its other names are *al-ḥanāna* "The Fretful," *al-hadūj* "The Moaner," *al-hawjāʾ* "The Tent-Uprooter," *al-khajawjāh* "The Dust-Up,"[40] and *al-ḍahūk* (?).[41]

♦

This might be where Ibn Khālawayh's text ends. Both manuscripts go on to conclude with a paraphrase of *al-Gharīb al-muṣannaf* (Uncommon Vocabulary, Arranged Systematically)

I.584–86 by Abū ʿUbayd, where most of the same words and definitions appear in a "Chapter of the Winds" (*Bāb al-Riyāḥ*), in roughly the same order.[42] The contents of this section could be someone's notes for private use, jotted into the blank space of an early manuscript of *On the names of the wind*, and inserted into the text by a subsequent copyist.

This is suggested by a couple of things, redundancy for one. Also, Ibn Khālawayh is distinguished for his pride in his sources, even when (like the ʿUmar b. al-Fatḥ named above) they are not well known. Nor can any aversion to crediting Abū ʿUbayd be detected elsewhere in his work (as in *K. Laysa*, 27).

But then there is the specification that "Ibn Khālawayh said" that *rāḥ* and *rayyiḥ* are epithets for windy days. In the whole section, these are some of the only words not to come from Abū ʿUbayd's chapter, and seem to be marked as insertions by Ibn Khālawayh himself. I have done nothing to emend this section.

♦

Al-īr and *al-hīr*, *al-ayr* and *al-hayr*, and *al-ayyir* and *al-hayyir* [might all mean something like "The Tumbler"].[43]

Al-nisʿ and *al-misʿ* "The Whippet,"[44] *al-zafāfa* "The Rustle,"[45] *al-ḥanūn* [cognate with *al-ḥanāna* above], *al-mujfil* and *al-jāfila* "The Dust-Raiser," *al-hajūm* "The Visitation," *al-bayyūt* "Confining People to their Tents," *al-naʾūj* and *al-nāja* "The Bawler," *al-sahūk*, *al-sayhūk*, *al-sahwaj*, and *al-sayhūj* [mentioned above], and *al-darūj* "The Treader" [are all winds' names].

Al-nasīm "The Breeze" and *al-nafḥ* "The Waft" are cool winds, and *al-lafḥ* "The Hot Gust" is a warm one.

[More winds' names:] *al-k͟hārim* "The Piercer," *al-sāfira* "The Sweeper," *al-habwa* "The Duster," *al-naḍīḍa* "The Soaker," *al-ḥawās͟hik* "The Swells," and *al-ʿariyya* "The Raw." *Al-hallāb* "The Bushy-Tailed" is a wind that brings rain. *Al-bawāriḥ* "The Bad Omens" are the hot north winds of summer.[46]

Ibn Khālawayh said: *Rāḥ* is said of a windy day, and feminine *rūḥa* of a windy night. A night which is *sākira* "inebriate" is windless. A day of pleasant winds is described as *rayyiḥ*.

Al-nāfija [the above-mentioned "Scatter"] is said for the wind when it first kicks up, and *al-hajūm* [the above-mentioned "Visitation"] for the wind whose force is strong enough to uproot tents and clumps of grass. *Al-naʾūj* [the above-mentioned "Bawler"] is another forceful wind. *Al-darūj* [the above-mentioned "Treader"] leaves a trail that looks like dragging reins.

Al-nasamān and *al-nasīm* are gentle breezes, and the verb *nasama tansimu* is said for the same. The verbs *ʿajja* "to raise a ruckus" and *asnafa* "to outpace" are said of forceful winds that set the dust in motion. Wind described as *khārim* "piercing" is cold wind.

Al-muʿṣirāt [are "whirling" winds that] usher in the rain. *Al-ḥawāshik* [the above-mentioned "Swells"] and *al-mushtarika* "The Minglers" are winds of varying strengths. *Al-ʿariyya* [the "raw wind" mentioned above] is a cold one. *Al-iʿṣār* [is the cyclone that] reaches up to the sky. *Al-ḥarjaf* [the "chill wind" mentioned above] is cold indeed.

♦

Here, with God's help, ends the treatise. Praise be to Him first and last, and upon our master Muḥammad, his family, and his companions be God's blessings and God's peace.[47]

NOTES

1 *Sūrat Āl ʿImrān* (The Family of ʿImrān) 3:117.

2 This rare hadith finds support in the Prophet's statement that "Two types of carrion are lawful for us: the fish and the locust," reported by Aḥmad b. Ḥanbal and others. But everywhere that "the locust killed by frost" is mentioned in hadith, it is with the contrary judgment—namely, that the locust killed by cold should *not* be eaten. Thus in *al-Mughnī* (The Summa) XIII.300 of Ibn Qudāma (d. 620/1223), the *Jāmiʿ li-aḥkām al-Qurʾān* (Collected Precepts on the Qurʾān) IV.177–78 of al-Qurṭubī (d. 671/1272) with reference to *Sūrat Āl ʿImrān* 3:117, and *Lisān* art. √*ṣrr*. In the present instance I would suspect a copyist's error, except that Ibn Khālawayh repeats the statement in *Sharḥ al-Maqṣūra*, 230.

3 *Sūrat Yūnus* (Jonah) 10:22.

4 *Sūrat al-Dhāriyāt* (Winnowing Winds) 51:41.

5 *Sūrat al-Anfāl* (Spoils of War) 8:46, *Sūrat al-Isrāʾ* (The Night Journey) 17:6.

6 These verses are attributed to Maysūn bt. Baḥdal, wife of the caliph Muʿāwiya b. Abī Sufyān (d. 60/680) and mother to his successor Yazīd (d. 64/683); see Zwettler (1993) and Hammond (2010), 116–17.

7 Abū l-Ḥasan ʿAlī b. Ḥāzim al-Liḥyānī was a lexicographer of Kufa who studied under Abū Zayd. None of his books have survived.

8 *Sūrat al-Aʿrāf* (The Heights) 7:57. The same idiom is in Isaiah, Hosea, and Psalms, noted by Rendsburg (1983).

9 *Sūrat Nūḥ* (Noah) 71:10–12.

10 *Sūrat al-Baqara* (The Cow) 2:15.

11 *Al-Muʾtafikāt* is also a Qurʾānic epithet for "The Overturned Cities" of Lot (as at 9:70, 69:9, and 53:53).

12 Both manuscripts have *al-nas̲h̲ʾ* in place of *al-nas̲h̲āṣ*. Although the former is attested as a word for "cloud," Sharaf's emendation to *nas̲h̲āṣ* is followed on the strength of the *Book of Rain*, which Ibn Khālawayh paraphrases here.

13 The expression "mother of all ____" drew ridicule outside the Arabic-speaking world after Saddam Hussein's warning that US military action in Iraq would end in "the mother of all battles." Lost in this word-for-word translation of *umm al-maʿārik* was the semantic reach of *umm*, which is not just the birth-giving parent, but the "exemplar" or "prototype" of its class. To call something an *umm* is to call it an emblematic case. This is the sense in which the winds have "mothers": they are the four cardinal templates for any wind that happens to blow.

14 The verses are attributed to Majnūn in *Aghānī* II.56 and *Dīwān Majnūn*, 57, but in *Dīwān al-maʿānī* I.274, Abū Hilāl al-ʿAskari (d. ca. 400/1010) says they're by Ibrahim b. al-ʿAbbās al-Ṣūlī

(d. after 244/858). Multiple attributions like this are common with Majnūn, whose poems are largely made up of verses by historical poets.

[15] Quoted by Ibn Qutayba, *Anwā'*, 163, and cobbled into a 6-verse poem in *Dīwān Kuthayyir*, 149–50.

[16] 'Āṣim b. Abī l-Nujūd (d. 127/745) was one of seven early reciters, along with Abū 'Amr (d. 154/770), whose versions of the Qur'ānic text are accepted to this day.

[17] Verse 24 of a 43-verse poem in the *dīwān* of al-A'shā (d. ca. 4/625), 115, quoted in Sībawayh's *Kitāb* I.30.

[18] *Sūrat al-Anbiyā'* (The Prophets) 21:81, *Sūrat Sabā'* (Sheba) 34:12, and *Sūrat Ṣād* (Ṣād) 38:36.

[19] This hadith couples the Muslim victory at the Battle of the Trench (5/627), where the enemy camp was overturned by winds, with the legendary destruction of 'Ād narrated in *Sūrat al-Aḥqāf* 46:24 (see ahead note 30).

[20] *Sūrat al-Baqara* 2:266. *Al-samūm* is discussed ahead at notes 32 and 33.

[21] That al-Maḥāmilī transmitted hadith directly from al-Dawraqī is affirmed in *Siyar a'lām al-nubalā'* (The Lives of Noble Individuals) XV.259 by al-Dhahabī (d. 748/1348), despite the gap of nearly eighty years between their death dates.

[22] This fable appears in *K. al-Maghāzī* (The Book of Expeditions) II.476 by al-Wāqidī (d. 207/822) with reference to the Battle of the Trench; also Abū l-Shaykh, *K. al-'Aẓama*, 287, and Ibn Abī l-Dunyā, *K. al-Maṭar*, 139.

[23] At Medina, the tribes of Aws and Khazraj were called the "Supporters" or "Helpers" (*al-Anṣār*) for their support of the Prophet's cause, and this is the origin of Abū Zayd's surname. Both tribes were considered newcomers to Medina, belonging to the South Arabian diaspora that fanned north in Late Antiquity, and Ibn Khālawayh says it was in this ancestral sense that the Prophet's help came from the direction of Yemen. Schimmel (1995), 28, mentions another interpretation that takes the "breath of Yemen" as an allusion to Uways al-Qaranī, the storied companion of the Prophet in Yemen who never entered Muḥammad's presence but communicated with him in dreams; see for starters Hussaini (1967) and Zakharia (1999). (The hadith itself is deemed unsound by the editors of Aḥmad b. Ḥanbal's *Musnad*, XVI.577n3.)

[24] These words for "North" all relate to *al-shimāl*, "the left hand," while the right hand (*al-yamīn*) relates to ease, good fortune and the South. Yemen was called in Latin *Arabia Felix*.

[25] *Al-jirbiyā'* is a cold wind, more often said to be a North or Northwest Wind than from the South. Its meaning is hard to tell. *Jarb* is "mange" and, formed on this this word, the feminine epithet *jarbā'* is applied to the night sky, as if it were lousy with stars (*Lisan* art. √*jrb*).

[26] *Qabūl* and *dabūr* are antonyms, defined against each other in various ways. One is that

the East Wind is called *al-Qabūl* because it "faces" (*tuqābilu*) the door to the Kaʿba, and *al-Dabūr* comes from its "rear" (*dubur*). The simplest explanation is in art. *qabl* of the *Qāmūs* (1045) of al-Fīrūzābādī (d. 817/1415): the East Wind is so called because the soul "turns to face it" (*li-anna al-nafs **taqbaluhā***), making *al-Dabūr* the wind you turn your back to.

27 Hämeen-Anttila (1996), 210. Quoted without attribution in Abū Zayd's *K. al-Nawādir*, 405, where *maḥwa* is defined as "a West Wind that scatters the clouds and sets them moving."

28 Verse 79 of a 126-verse poem in *Dīwān Dhī l-Rumma*, I.90.

29 *Al-kharīq* is said of hard and gentle winds equally, and for the wind of long continuous blowing as for the brief spell. Its formal relation to √*khrq* (a root of words for piercing and tearing) gives it two possible meanings: "The Ripper" and "The Rent." *Lisān* art. √*khrq* cites the latter meaning from al-Azharī's *Tahdhīb*, art. √*khrq*: "*Al-kharīq* names a cold wind that blows forcefully, as if punctured (*ka-annahā khuriqat*)."

30 *Al-ṣarṣar* for the wind is heard in the Qurʾān at 41:16, 54:19, and 69:6. Lexicographers connect it either to *ṣirr* (the word for "frost" already mentioned), or to the verb *ṣarṣara*, used for all kinds of monotonous racket. *Ṣarṣār* are crickets.

31 *Al-hāriya* is how this word appears in manuscript (fol. 2v7), and nowhere else. Sharaf (74n2) mentions two words that could possibly have been miswritten as *al-hāriya* (الهارية): "*Lisān* art. √*hdy* quotes al-Aṣmaʿī to the effect that *al-hādiya* (الهادية) of a thing is its 'foremost part,' and *al-qāriya* (القارية) is a 'bladed edge,' as of a spearhead or a sword." Neither is attested elsewhere as a name of the wind.

32 *Al-samūm* is formally related to *al-samm*, the noun for "poison" and the act of poisoning. To what extent the name for wind connotes this idea is debatable. *Samūm* is more the name of a specific wind than a descriptive epithet, though *Lisān* art. √*smm* says it can be either (*isman wa-ṣifatan*). For the "sandstorm," *samūm* is postclassical usage (according to Lane's *Arabic-English Lexicon* IV.1420, art. √*smm*), and has become naturalized in modern European languages (for example, English *simoom*).

33 Elsewhere, a different judgment on the matter is attributed to al-Farrāʾ: "*Al-ḥarūr* can happen any time, but *al-samūm* happens only by day." Thus in al-Qurṭubī's *Jāmiʿ* XIV.339 with reference to *Sūrat al-Fāṭir* (The Creator) 35:21, where the poet Ruʾba is said to have opined contrarily that *ḥarūr* belongs to day and *samūm* to night.

34 Ibn Khālawayh quotes this hadith in *Sharḥ al-Maqṣūra*, 311, there as here on the authority of ʿUmar b. al-Fatḥ al-Baghdādī, a person who is barely known (Ibn al-Najjār, *Dhayl Tārīkh Baghdād* XX.93–94).

35 The Prophet's dread of wind is reported elsewhere, always by his wife ʿĀʾisha: "Whenever he spotted a raincloud or sensed a wind, it would show on his face. 'O Prophet of God,' I said to him, 'I see other people rejoicing when they spot a cloud, in expectation that it holds rain, but when you spot the cloud, I recognize displeasure on your face.' He said: 'O ʿĀʾisha, it brings me no reassurance, for I know what punishment may be in it. Destruction came to one people in the form of a wind, who when they saw it approaching, said: "Here we have a cloud-bank that brings rain."'" Reported by al-Bukhārī (d. 256/870) and Muslim (d. 261/875) in their chapters on Qurʾānic commentary with reference to *Sūrat al-Aḥqāf* (The Dunes) 46:24.

36 *Al-sakīna* is from Hebrew *Shekhinah*, a postbiblical word for the indwelling presence of God; see for an overview Fahd (1995). At *Sūrat al-Baqara* 2:248, it is said to dwell within the Ark of the Covenant (*al-Tābūt*). Where it is described as a cat with wings, as in the *Tafsīr* (Commentary) of al-Ṭabarī (d. 310/923) V.327–28, it seems to indicate a sphinx. This harmonizes with biblical descriptions of Solomon's Temple, whose inner sanctuary was decorated with sphinxes (Hebrew *keruvim*), as was the Ark itself (Exodus 26:18–22, I Kings 6:23–25).

37 By omitting the chain of transmitters (which this hadith has in *K. al-ʿAẓama*, 287–88 and Ibn Abī l-Dunyā's *K. al-Maṭar*, 148–49), Ibn Khālawayh appears to concede its lack of soundness. The ending recalls *Iliad* 20.74: "The river that mortals call *Scamander* is called *Xanthos* by the gods."

38 *Al-ʿurf* is also said for the rooster's crest and the lion's mane. Its plural, *al-Aʿrāf* (The Heights), is the title of the seventh *sūra* of the Qurʾān, and the poem "Al Aaraaf" (1829) by Edgar Allan Poe.

39 The editors of *K. al-ʿAẓama*, 272, and Ibn Abī l-Dunyā's *K. al-Maṭar*, 140, call the hadith apocryphal. As narrators, ʿUbays and Abū l-Muhazzam are rated *matrūk* (to be rejected).

40 For *al-khajawjāh* and its affiliated wind-words there are as many definitions as you please. When this happens, the trick is to look elsewhere within the same root for ideas. *Lisān* art. √*khjj* defines *al-khajj* as the tread that raises dust from the ground, and also a defensive blow (*al-dafʿ*).

41 The Cairo manuscript (fol. 3r9) has *al-ḍahūk*, an unknown word emended by Sharaf (81n5) to *al-sahūk*, even though *al-sahūk* occurs just ahead (fol. 3r12).

42 Noted in the edition of Ḍāmin (1974), 225n51.

43 The wind called by these names is variously defined as an East Wind, a North Wind, a Northwest Wind, or a Southwest one. It seems to be related to *al-hīr*, which is related to verbs for the "collapse" of a cliff or an edifice, and just as well to *al-hayra*, "a level plain" (*Lisān* art. √*hyr*).

44 "The North Wind called *nisʿ* gets its name from the fineness of its blowing, as likened to the braided thong of leather called *al-nisʿ*," says al-Azharī in *Tahdhīb* art. √*nsʿ*.

45 *Zafzāfa*, not *zafāfa*, is how this word appears in *al-Gharīb al-muṣannaf*, unaltered here.

46 *Lisān* art. √*brḥ* cites Abū Zayd to the effect that *bawāriḥ* (sg. *bāriḥ* and *bāriḥa*) are rainless North winds exclusive to summer, noting that "al-Azharī said [in *Tahdhīb* V.28, art. √*brḥ*]: 'The speech of my Arab informants agrees with what Abū Zayd says about it.'"

47 The St. Petersburg manuscript ends with a statement by al-Qūṣūnī: "Copied after evening prayers on 7 Rabīʿ II of the year 1003 (December 10, 1594). May God make fast its seal."

SOURCES

I. THE *BOOK OF RAIN*

Bibliothèque nationale de France MS 4231 Arabe (dated 631/1233-4), fol. 1v–14r, in two published editions:

1. Edited by R. J. H. Gottheil (1896). *Journal of the American Oriental Society* 16: 282–317.
2. Edited by Louis Cheikho (1905). Beirut: Imprimerie Catholique; reprinted in *al-Bulgha fī shudhūr al-lugha / Dix anciens traités de philologie arabe*, ed. Auguste Haffner and Louis Cheikho (Beirut: Imprimerie Catholique, 1908), 99–120.

II. OTHER PUBLISHED TEXTS OF ABŪ ZAYD

"al-Mukhtār min *K. al-Amthāl*," ed. Jalīl al-ʿAṭiyya (1986). *al-Mawrid* 15:2, 77–86.

K. al-Hamz, traité philologique inédit, ed. Louis Cheikho (1911). Beirut: Imprimerie Catholique.

K. al-Libāʾ wa-al-laban, ed. Louis Cheikho (1908). *Al-Bulgha fī shudhūr al-lugha / Dix anciens traités de philologie arabe*, ed. Auguste Haffner and Louis Cheikho. Beirut: Imprimerie Catholique, 141–45.

K. al-Nawādir fī al-lugha:

1. Edited by Saʿīd al-Khūrī Shartūnī (1894). Beirut: Imprimerie Catholique; repr. Beirut: Dār al-Kitāb al-ʿArabī, 1967.
2. Edited by Muḥammad ʿAbd al-Qādir Aḥmad (1981). Beirut: Dār al-Shurūq.
3. Edited by Muḥammad ʿUthmān and Emil Badīʿ Yaʿqūb (2011). Beirut: Dār al-Kutub al-ʿIlmiyya.

K. al-Shajar wa-al-kalā':

1. Edited by Samuel Nagelberg (1909). *Kitâb aš-šağar: Ein botansiches Lexikon.* Kirchhain (Germany): Max Schmersow.
2. Edited by Anwar Abū Suwaylim and Muḥammad 'Alī al-Shawābika (1995). *K. al-Shajar wa-al-kalā'.* 'Ammān: Dār al-Abjadiyya.

III. APPENDIX: *ON THE NAMES OF THE WIND*

St. Petersburg State University MS O 839 (dated 1003/1594), fol. 28v–30r, in two editions:

1. "Ibn Ḫālawaih's *Kitāb al-Rīḥ*," ed. Ignaz Kratchkovsky (1926). *Islamica* 2:3, 331–43.
2. "*Risāla Fī asmā' al-rīḥ* li-Ibn Khālawayh," ed. Ḥātim Ṣāliḥ al-Ḍāmin (1974). *al-Mawrid* 3:4, 220–32.

Cairo, Dār al-Kutub MS 5252 ﻫ (nineteenth century?), fol. 1r–3r, in one edition:

3. *al-Rīḥ*, ed. Ḥusayn Muḥammad Muḥammad Sharaf (1984). Medina: Mu'assasat al-Ḥalabī lī-l-Ṭibā'a wa-l-Nashr.

IV. PRIMARY SOURCES

'Abīd b. al-Abraṣ (1994). *Dīwān 'Abīd b. al-Abraṣ*, ed. Ashraf Aḥmad 'Adra. Beirut: Dār al-Kitāb al-'Arabī. Series title: Shu'arā'unā.

Abū Dhu'ayb al-Hudhalī (1998). *Dīwān Abī Dhu'ayb al-Hudhalī*, ed. Sūhām al-Miṣrī and Yāsīn al-Ayyūbī. Beirut: al-Maktab al-Islamī.

Abū l-Ṭayyib al-Lughawī (1955). *Marātib al-naḥwiyyīn*, ed. Muḥammad Abū l-Faḍl Ibrāhīm. Cairo: Maktabat Nahḍat Miṣr.

Abū 'Ubayd al-Qāsim b. Sallām (1984–1999). *Gharīb al-ḥadīth*, ed. Ḥusayn Muḥammad Muḥammad Sharaf et al. Cairo: al-Hay'a al-'Āmma li-Shu'ūn al-Maṭābi' al-Amīriyya. (5 vols. + index.)

——— (2005). *al-Gharīb al-muṣannaf*, ed. Ṣafwān 'Adnān Dāwūdī. Damascus: Dār al-Fayḥā'. (2 vols. + index.)

'Adiyy b. al-Riqā' (1987). *Dīwān shi'r 'Adiyy b. al-Riqā' al-'Āmilī*, ed. Nūrī Ḥamūdī al-Qaysī and Ḥātim Ṣāliḥ al-Ḍāmin. Baghdad: Maṭba'at al-Majma' al-'Ilmī al-'Irāqī.

al-'Ajjāj, 'Abd Allāh b. Ru'ba (1971). *Dīwān al-'Ajjāj, riwāyat 'Abd al-Malik b. Qurayb al-Aṣma'ī*, ed. 'Izzat Ḥasan. Beirut: Maktabat Dār al-Sharq.

al-Aʿshā, Maymūn b. Qays [1950]. *Dīwān al-Aʿshā al-Kabīr*. Cairo: Maktabat al-Adab.

al-ʿAskarī, Abū Hilāl (AH 1352 = 1933). *Dīwān al-maʿānī*. Cairo: Maktabat al-Qudsī. (2 vols.)

al-Dhahabī, Shams al-Dīn Muḥammad (1996). *Siyar aʿlām al-nubalāʾ*, ed. Shuʿayb al-Arnaʾūṭ et al. Beirut: Muʾassasat al-Risāla. (25 vols.)

Dhū l-Rumma (1982). *Dīwān Dhī l-Rumma, Ghaylān b. ʿUqba al-ʿAdawī al-mutawaffā fī sanat 117 H.; sharḥ al-Imām Abī Naṣr Aḥmad b. Ḥātim al-Bāhilī, ṣāḥib al-Aṣmaʿī; Riwāyat al-Imām Abī l-ʿAbbās Thaʿlab*, ed. ʿAbd al-Quddūs Abū Ṣāliḥ. 2nd ed. Beirut: Muʾassasat al-Risāla. (3 vols.)

al-Fārābī, Abū Naṣr (1996). *Iḥṣāʾ al-ʿulūm*, ed. ʿAlī Abū Mulḥim. Beirut: Dār wa-Maktabat al-Hilāl.

al-Fīrūzābādī (2005). *al-Qāmūs al-muḥīṭ*, ed. Muḥammad Naʿīm al-ʿAraqsūsī et al. Beirut: Muʾassasat al-Risāla. 8th printing. (1 vol.)

Ibn Abī l-Dunyā (1997). *Kitāb al-Maṭar wa-al-raʿd wa-al-barq wa-al-rīḥ*, ed. Ṭāriq Muḥammad al-ʿUmūdī. Riyadh: Dār al-Jawzī.

Ibn al-Aʿrābī, Muḥammad b. Ziyād (1970). *K. al-Biʾr*, ed. Ramaḍān ʿAbd al-Tawwāb. Cairo: al-Hayʾa al-Miṣriyya al-ʿĀmma li-l-Taʾlīf wa-l-Nashr.

Ibn al-Dumayna [1959]. *Dīwān Ibn al-Dumayna, ṣanʿat Abī l-ʿAbbās Thaʿlab wa-Muḥammad ibn Ḥabīb*, ed. Aḥmad Rātib al-Naffākh. Cairo: Maktabat Dār al-ʿUrūba.

Ibn Durayd, Abū Bakr Muḥammad (1963). *Kitāb Waṣf al-maṭar wa-al-saḥāb*, ed. ʿIzz al-Dīn al-Tanūkhī. Damascus: al-Majmaʿ al-ʿIlmī al-ʿArabī.

Ibn Ḥajar al-ʿAsqalānī (1968). *Tahdhīb al-Tahdhīb*. Beirut: Dār Ṣādir. (12 vols.)

Ibn Ḥanbal, Aḥmad (1995–2001). *Musnad al-Imām Aḥmad b. Ḥanbal*. Beirut: Muʾassasat al-Risāla. (50 vols.)

Ibn Harma al-Qurashī (1969). *Shiʿr Ibn Harma al-Qurashī*, ed. Muḥammad Naffāʿ and Ḥusayn ʿAṭwān. Damascus: Majmaʿ al-Lugha al-ʿArabiyya.

Ibn Isḥāq and Ibn Hishām (1936). *al-Sīra al-nabawiyya*, ed. Muṣṭafā al-Saqqā, Ibrāhīm al-Abyārī, and ʿAbd al-Ḥafīẓ Shalabī. Cairo: Maṭbaʿat Muṣṭafā al-Bābī al-Ḥalabī. (4 vols.)

Ibn Jinnī, Abū l-Fatḥ ʿUthmān (1952–1956). *al-Khaṣāʾiṣ*, ed. Muḥammad ʿAlī al-Najjār. Cairo: Maṭbaʿat Dār al-Kutub al-Miṣriyya. (3 vols.)

Ibn Kathīr, Ismāʿīl b. ʿUmar (1998). *The Life of Muḥammad*, tr. Trevor le Gassick. Reading, UK: Garnet Publishing. (4 vols.)

Ibn Khālawayh, al-Ḥusayn b. Aḥmad (2000). *K. Laysa fī kalām al-'arab*, ed. Dīzīrih Saqqāl. Beirut: Dār al-Fikr al-'Arabī.

——— (2017). *Names of the Lion*, tr. David Larsen. Seattle: Wave Books.

——— (1986). *Sharḥ Maqṣūrat Ibn Durayd*. In Maḥmūd Jāsim Muḥammad, *Ibn Khālawayh wa-juhūduhu fī al-lugha, ma'a taḥqīq* K. Sharḥ Maqṣūrat Ibn Durayd. Beirut: Mu'assasat al-Risāla.

Ibn Khallikān, Abū l-'Abbās Aḥmad (1998). *Wafayāt al-a'yān wa-anbā' abnā' al-zamān*, ed. Yūsuf 'Alī Ṭawīl and Maryam Qāsim Ṭawīl. Beirut: Dar al-Kutub al-'Ilmiyya. (6 vols.)

Ibn Mujāhid, Abū Bakr (1972). *K. al-Sab'a fī al-qirā'āt*, ed. Shawqī Ḍayf. Cairo: Dār al-Ma'ārif bi-Miṣr.

(Ibn) al-Nadīm, Abū l-Faraj Muḥammad (2009). *al-Fihrist*, ed. Ayman Fu'ād Sayyid. London: Mu'assasat al-Furqān li-l Turāth al-Islāmī. (2 vols. in 4.)

Ibn al-Najjār al-Baghdādī (2004). *Dhayl Tārīkh Baghdād*. Vols. 16–20 of al-Khaṭīb al-Baghdādī, *Tārīkh Baghdād aw Madīnat al-Salām*, ed. Muṣṭafā 'Abd al-Qādir 'Aṭā. Beirut: Dār al-Kutub al-'Ilmiyya.

Ibn Qudāma al-Maqdisī (1992). *al-Mughnī*, ed. 'Abd Allāh b. 'Abd al-Muḥsin al-Turki and 'Abd al-Fattāḥ Muḥammad al-Ḥulw. Cairo: Hujr li-l-Ṭibā'a wa-l-Nashr. 2nd ed. (15 vols.)

Ibn Qutayba, 'Abd Allāh b. Muslim (1982). *Adab al-kātib*, ed. Muḥammad al-Dālī. Beirut: Mu'assasat al-Risāla.

——— (1978). *Kitāb al-Anwā' fī mawāsim al-'arab*. Hyderabad: Dā'irat al-Ma'ārif al-'Uthmāniyya. Reprint.

——— (1966). *al-Shi'r wa-al-shu'arā'*, ed. Muḥammad Yūsuf Najm and Iḥsān 'Abbās. Beirut: Dār al-Thaqāfa, 1964. (2 vols.)

——— (1966). *Ta'wīl mukhtalif al-ḥadīth*, ed. Muḥammad Zuhrī al-Najjār. Cairo: Maktabat al-Kulliyyāt al-Azhariyya.

Ibn Rashīq al-Qayrawānī (2000). *al-'Umda fī ṣinā'at al-shi'r*, ed. al-Nabawī 'Abd al-Wāḥid Sha'lān. Cairo: Maktabat al-Khānjī. (2 vols.)

Ibn al-Shajarī, Hibat Allāh b. 'Alī al-Baghdādī (1970). *al-Ḥamāsa al-Shajariyya*, ed. 'Abd al-Mu'īn al-Mallūḥī and Asmā' al-Ḥimṣī. Damascus: Manshūrāt Wizārat al Thaqāfa. (2 vols.)

Imru' al-Qays (2000). *Dīwān Imri' al-Qays wa-mulḥaqātuhu, sharḥ Abī Sa'īd al-Sukkarī*, ed. Anwar Abū Suwaylim and Muḥammad 'Alī al-Shawābika. Al Ain (UAE): Markaz Zāyid li-l-Turāth wa-l-Tārīkh. (2 vols.)

al-Iṣbahānī, Abū l-Faraj (2008). *Kitāb al-Aghānī*, ed. Iḥsān 'Abbās, Ibrāhīm al-Sa'āfīn, and Bakr 'Abbās. Beirut: Dār Ṣādir. (25 vols.)

al-Iṣbahānī, Abū l-Shaykh b. Ḥayyān (1994). *K. al-'Aẓama*, ed. Muḥammad Fāris. Beirut: Dār al-Kutub al-'Ilmiyya.

Jābir b. Ḥayyān (1935). *Mukhtār rasā'il Jābir b. Ḥayyān*, ed. Paul Kraus. Paris and Cairo: G. P. Maisonneuve / Maktabat al-Khānjī.

al-Jāḥiẓ, 'Amr b. Baḥr (1968). *al-Bayān wa-al-tabyīn*, ed. 'Abd al-Salām Muḥammad Hārūn. Cairo and Beirut: Maktabat al-Khānjī / Maktabat al-Hilāl. (4 vols.)

——— (1938–1965). *Kitāb al-Ḥayawān*, ed. 'Abd al-Salām Muḥammad Hārūn. Cairo: Maktabat Muṣṭafā al-Bābī al-Ḥalabī. (7 vols.)

al-Khālidiyyān, Abū Bakr Muḥammad and Abū 'Uthmān Sa'īd (1958–65). *Kitāb al-Ashbāh wa-al-naẓā'ir min ash'ār al-mutaqaddimīn wa-al-jāhiliyyati wa-al-mukhaḍramīn li-al-Khālidiyyayn*, ed. al-Sayyid Muḥammad Yūsuf. Cairo: Lajnat al-Ta'līf wa-l-Tarjama wa-l-Nashr. (2 vols.)

al-Khalīl b. Aḥmad (2002). *Kitāb al-'Ayn, murattaban 'alā ḥurūf al-mu'jam*, ed. 'Abd al-Ḥamīd Hindāwī. Beirut: Dār al-Kutub al-'Ilmiyya. (4 vols.) Series title: Manshūrāt Muḥammad 'Alī Bayḍūn.

al-Khansā', Tumāḍir bt. 'Amr b. al-Ḥārith (1988). *Dīwān al-Khansā', sharaḥahu Tha'lab*, ed. Anwar Abū Suwaylim. Amman: Dār 'Ammār.

al-Khaṭīb al-Baghdādī (2004). *Tārīkh Baghdād aw Madīnat al-Salām*, ed. Muṣṭafā 'Abd al-Qādir 'Aṭā. Beirut: Dār al-Kutub al-'Ilmiyya. (24 vols.)

al-Khaṭṭābī al-Bustī (1982–1983). *Gharīb al-ḥadīth*, ed. 'Abd al-Karīm Ibrāhīm al-'Azabāwī. Mecca: Markaz al-Baḥth al-'Ilmī wa-Iḥyā' al-Turāth al-Islāmī, Jāmi'at Umm al-Qurā. (3 vols.) Series title: Min al-Turāth al-'Arabī, no. 17.

al-Kindī, Ya'qūb b. Isḥāq (1953). *Rasā'il al-Kindī al-falsafiyya*, ed. Muḥammad 'Abdalhādī Abū Rīda. Cairo: Dār al-Fikr al-'Arabī. (2 vols. in 1.); repr. Frankfurt am Main: Institute for the History of Arabic-Islamic Science, 1999.

——— (2000). *Scientific Weather Forecasting in the Middle Ages: The Writings of al-Kindī.*

Studies, Editions, and Translations of the Arabic, Hebrew and Latin Texts, ed. and tr. by Gerrit Bos and Charles Burnett. London and New York: Kegan Paul International. Series title: The Sir Henry Wellcome Asian Series.

al-Kumayt al-Asadī (2000). *Dīwān al-Kumayt b. Zayd al-Asadī*, ed. Muḥammad Nabīl al-Ṭarīfī. Beirut: Dār Ṣādir.

Kuthayyir ʿAzza (1971). *Dīwān Kuthayyir ʿAzza*, ed. Iḥsān ʿAbbās. Beirut: Dār al-Thaqāfa.

Labīd b. Rabīʿa (1962). *Sharḥ Dīwān Labīd b. Rabīʿa*, ed. Iḥsān ʿAbbās. Kuwait: Wizārat al-Irshād wa-l-inbāʾ. Series title: al-Turāth al-ʿArabī, no. 8.

al-Lablī, Abū Jaʿfar Aḥmad b. Yūsuf (1997). *Tuḥfat al-majd al-ṣarīḥ fī* Sharḥ K. al-Faṣīḥ, ed. ʿAbd al-Malik al-Thabītī. Cairo: Maktabat al-Ādāb.

Majnūn Laylā, Qays b. al-Mulawwaḥ [1979]. *Dīwān Majnūn Laylā*, ed. ʿAbd al-Sattār Aḥmad Farrāj. Cairo: Dār Miṣr li-l-Ṭibāʿa. Series title: Maṭbūʿāt Maktabat Miṣr.

al-Marzūqī, Abū ʿAlī Aḥmad b. Muḥammad (1995). *Kitāb al-Amālī*, ed. Yaḥyā Wahīb al-Jubūrī. Beirut: Dār al-Gharb al-Islāmī.

——— (1996). *Kitāb al-Azmina wa-l-amkina*, ed. Khalīl al-Manṣūr. Beirut: Dār al-Kutub al-ʿIlmiyya.

al-Mufaḍḍal al-Ḍabbī [1979]. *al-Mufaḍḍaliyyāt*, ed. Aḥmad Muḥammad Shākir and ʿAbd al-Salām Muḥammad Hārūn. Cairo: Dār al-Maʿārif. 6th printing.

al-Murtaḍā, ʿAlī ibn al-Ḥusayn (1954). *Amālī al-Murtaḍā: Ghurar al-fawāʾid wa-durar al-qalāʾid*, ed. Muḥammad Abū l-Faḍl Ibrāhīm. Cairo: Dār Iḥyāʾ al-Kutub al-ʿArabiyya / ʿĪsā al-Bābī al-Ḥalabī. (2 vols.)

al-Nābigha al-Dhubyānī (1985). *Dīwān al-Nābigha*, ed. Muḥammad Abu al-Faḍl Ibrāhīm. Cairo: Dār al-Maʿārif. 2nd printing. Series title: Dhakhāʾir al-ʿArab, 25.

Novalis (1967). *Gesammelte Werke*, ed. Hildberg and Werner Kohlschmidt. Gütersloh: Sigbert Mohn.

al-Qāḍī ʿAbd al-Jabbār al-Asadābādī (1961). *al-Mughnī fī abwāb al-tawḥīd wa-al-ʿadl*, vol. 7: *Khalq al-Qurʾān*, ed. Ibrāhīm al-Abyārī and Ṭāhā Ḥusayn. [Cairo]: al-Muʾassasat al-Miṣriyya al-ʿĀmma li-l-Taʾlīf wa-l-Anbāʾ wa-l-Nashr.

al-Qāḍī al-Quḍāʿī (2013). *A Treasury of Virtues: Sayings, Sermons and Teachings of ʿAlī*, ed. and tr. Tahera Qutbuddin. New York: NYU Press. Series title: Library of Arabic Literature.

al-Qifṭī, Jamāl al-Dīn ʿAlī b. Yūsuf (1986). *Inbāh al-ruwāt ʿalā anbāh al-nuḥḥāt*, ed. Muḥammad Abū l-Faḍl Ibrāhīm. Cairo and Beirut: Dār al-Fikr al-ʿArabī / Mu'assasat al-Kutub al Thaqāfiyya. (4 vols.)

al-Qurṭubī, Muḥammad b. Aḥmad (1967). *al-Jāmiʿ li-aḥkām al-Qurʾān*, ed. Hishām Samīr al-Bukhārī. Cairo: Dār al-Kātib al-ʿArabī li-l-Ṭibāʿa wa-l-Nashr. (20 vols.)

al-Qūṣūnī, Madyan b. ʿAbd al-Raḥmān (1979–1980). *Qāmūs al-aṭibbāʾ wa-nāmūs al-alibbāʾ*, ed. Ḥusnī Ṣubḥ. Damascus: Majmaʿ al-Lugha al-ʿArabiyya. (2 vols.)

Quṭrub, Abū ʿAlī Muḥammad al-Mustanīr (1985). *Kitab al-Azmina wa-talbiyat al-jāhiliyya*, ed. Ḥātim Ṣāliḥ al-Ḍāmin. Beirut: Mu'assasat al-Risāla.

Ru'ba b. al-ʿAjjāj (1903). *Der Dīwān des Reǧezdichters Rūba ben elʿAǧǧāǧ*, ed. Wilhelm Ahlwardt. Berlin: Verlag von Reuther & Reichard. Series title: Sammlungen alter arabischer Dichter, vol. 3.

al-Shāfiʿī, Muḥammad b. Idrīs (2013). *The Epistle on Legal Theory*, ed. and tr. by Joseph E. Lowry. New York: NYU Press. Series title: Library of Arabic Literature.

al-Sukkarī, Abī Saʿīd [1963–1965]. *Kitāb Sharḥ ashʿār al-Hudhaliyīn, ṣanʿat Abī Saʿīd al-Ḥasan b. al-Ḥusayn al-Sukkarī*, ed. ʿAbd al-Sattār Aḥmad Farrāj and Maḥmūd Muḥammad Shākir. Cairo: Maktabat Dār al-ʿUrūba. (3 vols.) Series title: Kunūz al-Shiʿr, no. 3.

al-Suyūṭī, Jalāl al-Dīn (1976). *Kitāb al-Iqtirāḥ fī ʿilm uṣūl al-naḥw*, ed. Aḥmad Muḥammad Qāsim. Cairo: s.n.

——— (1971). *al-Muzhir fī ʿulūm al-lugha*, ed. Muḥammad Aḥmad Jād al-Mawlā, ʿAlī Muḥammad al-Bajāwī, and Muḥammad Abū l-Faḍl Ibrāhīm. Cairo: Dār Iḥyāʾ al-Kutub al-ʿArabiyya / ʿĪsā al-Bābī al-Ḥalabī wa-Shurakāhu. (2 vols.)

al-Ṭabarī, Muḥammad b. Jarīr (1961–1969). *Tafsīr al-Ṭabarī: Jāmiʿ al-bayān ʿan taʾwīl āy al-Qurʾān*, ed. Maḥmūd and Aḥmad Muḥammad Shākir. Cairo: Dār al-Maʿārif. (16 vols.)

Tamīm b. Muqbil (1995). *Dīwān Ibn Muqbil*, ed. ʿIzzat Ḥasan. Beirut and Aleppo: Dār al-Sharaf al-ʿArabī.

Ṭayfūr, Aḥmad ibn Abī Ṭāhir (1998). *Balāghāt al-nisāʾ*, ed. ʿAbd al-Ḥamīd Hindāwī. Cairo: Dār al-Faḍīla.

Thaʿlab, Abū l-ʿAbbās Aḥmad b. Yaḥyā [1960]. *Majālis Thaʿlab*, ed. ʿAbd al-Salām Hārūn. Cairo: Dār al-Maʿārif bi-Miṣr. 2nd edition.

Thesiger, Wilfred (1960). *Arabian Sands*. London: Readers Union / Longman's, Green & Co.

al-Tirmidhī, ʿAbū Īsā b. ʿĪsā (1965–1967). *Sunan al-Tirmidhī, wa-huwa al-Jāmiʿ al-ṣaḥīḥ*, ed. ʿAbd al-Raḥmān Muḥammad ʿUthmān. Medina: al-Maktaba al-Salafiyya. (5 vols.)

al-ʿUqaylī, Abū Jaʿfar Muḥammad b. ʿAmr (1984). *Kitāb al-Ḍuʿafāʾ al-Kabīr*, ed. ʿAbd al-Muʿṭī Amīn Qalʿajī. Beirut: Dār al-Kutub al-ʿIlmiyya. (4 vols.)

al-Wāqidī, Muḥammad b. ʿUmar (1966). *Kitāb al-Maghāzī*, ed. Marsden Jones. London and Cairo: Oxford University Press / Dār al-Maʿārif bi-Miṣr. (3 vols.)

Yāqūt al-Ḥamawī (1977). *Muʿjam al-buldān*. Beirut: Dār Ṣādir. (5 vols.)

——— (1993). *Muʿjam al-udabāʾ*, ed. Iḥsān ʿAbbās. Beirut: Dār al-Gharb al-Islāmī (7 vols.)

al-Zabīdī, al-Murtaḍā (1965–2001). *Tāj al-ʿarūs min jawāhir al-Qāmūs*, ed. ʿAbd al-Sattār Aḥmad Farrāj et al. Kuwait: Maṭbaʿat Ḥukūmat al-Kuwayt / Muʾassasat al-Kuwayt li-al-Taqdīm al-ʿIlmī. (40 vols.)

al-Zamakhsharī, Jār Allāh b. ʿUmar (1966–1968). *Kashshāf ḥaqāʾiq al-tanzīl wa-ʿuyūn al-aqāwīl fī wujūh al-taʾwīl*. Cairo: Muṣṭafā al-Bābī al-Ḥalabī. (4 vols.)

al-Zawzanī, Ḥusayn b. Aḥmad (1972). *Sharḥ al-Muʿallaqāt al-sabʿ*. Beirut: Dār Ṣādir.

Zuhayr b. Abī Sulmā (1982). *Sharḥ shiʿr Zuhayr b. Abī Sulmā, ṣanʿat Abī l-ʿAbbās Thaʿlab*, ed. Fakhr al-Dīn Qabāwa. Beirut: Dār al-Āfāq al-Jadīda.

V. SECONDARY SOURCES

Abū Suwaylim, Anwar (1987). *al-Maṭar fī al-shiʿr al-jāhilī*. Amman and Beirut: Dār ʿAmmār / Dār al-Jīl.

Aḥmad, Muḥammad ʿAbd al-Qādir (1980). *Abū Zayd al-Anṣārī wa-*Nawādir al-lugha. Cairo and Beirut: Maktabat al-Nahḍa al-Miṣriyya / Dār al-Shurūq.

Albright, William F. (1920). "Gilgames and Engidu, Mesopotamian Genii of Fecundity." *Journal of the American Oriental Society* 40: 307–35.

Allen, Richard Hinckley (1899). *Star-Names and Their Meanings*. New York: G. E. Stechert.

Arnaldez, Roger, and Louis Massignon (1963). "Arabic Science." *Ancient and Medieval Science from the Beginnings to 1450*, ed. René Taton, tr. A. J. Pomerans. New York: Basic Books.

Assmann, Aleida (2011). *Cultural Memory and Western Civilization: Functions, Media, Archives*. Cambridge: Cambridge University Press.

Assmann, Jan (2010). *The Price of Monotheism*, tr. Robert Savage. Stanford: Stanford University Press.

al-ʿAṭiyya, Khalīl Ibrāhīm (1990). *Lughawiyyūn baṣriyyun: Abū Zayd al-Anṣārī wa-kitabuhu* al-Hamz. Basra: Dār al-Ḥikma, Jāmiʿat al-Baṣra. Series title: Silsilat Turāth al-Baṣra, no. 5.

Baalbaki, Ramzi (2014), *The Arabic Lexicographical Tradition from the 2nd/8th to the 12th/18th Century*. Leiden and Boston: Brill.

——— (2011). "The Historical Relevance of Poetry in the Arab Grammatical Tradition." *Poetry and History: The Value of Poetry in Reconstructing Arab History*, ed. Baalbaki, Saleh Said Agha, and Tarif Khalidi. Beirut: AUB Press. 95–120.

Bakhtin, Mikhail (1986). *Speech Genres and Other Essays*, ed. Michael Holquist and Caryl Emerson, tr. Vern W. McGee. Austin: University of Texas Press. Series title: University of Texas Press Slavic Series.

Bauer, Thomas (1994). "Die Pflanzensystematik der Araber." *XXV. Deutscher Orientalistentag vom 8. bis 13.4.1991 in München: Vorträge*, ed. Cornelia Wunsch. Stuttgart: Franz Steiner Verlag. 108–17.

Boiy, Tom and Kris Verhoeven (1998). "Arrian, *Anabasis* VII 21.2–4 and the Pallukkatu Channel." *Changing Watercourses in Babylonia*, ed. Hermann Gasche and Michel Tanret. Ghent and Chicago: University of Ghent / Oriental Institute of the University of Chicago. Vol. 1, 147–58.

Bräunlich, Erich (1926). *The Well in Ancient Arabia*. Leipzig: Verlag der Asia Minor.

Carter, Michael G. (1990). "Arabic Lexicography." *Religion, Learning and Science in the ʿAbbāsid Period*, ed. M. J. L. Young et al. Cambridge: Cambridge University Press. 106–17.

Chuine, Isabelle, et al. (2004). "Grape ripening as a past climate indicator." *Nature* 432: 289–90.

Cichocki, Piotr, and Marcin Kilarski (2010). "On 'Eskimo Words for Snow': The life cycle of a linguistic misconception." *Historiographia Linguistica* 37:3, 341–77.

Conger, George P. (1952). "Did India Influence Early Greek Philosophies?" *Philosophy East and West* 2:2, 102–28.

Corriente, Federico (1976). "From Old Arabic to Classical Arabic Through the Pre-Islamic Koine: Some Notes on the Native Grammarians' Sources, Attitudes and Goals." *Journal of Semitic Studies* 21:1/2, 62–98.

Coşeriu, Eugenio (1961). *¿Arabismos o romanismos?* Montevideo: Universidad de la República, Facultad de Humanidades y Ciencias (Departamento de Lingüistica).

Cusk, Rachel (1997). *The Country Life*. London: Picador; pb ed. Faber & Faber, 2019.

Daiber, Hans (1992). "The *Meteorology* of Theophrastus and Syriac and Arabic Translation." *Theophrastus: His Psychological, Doxographical, and Scientific Writings*, ed. William W. Fortenbaugh and Dimitri Gutas. New Brunswick, NJ and London: Transaction Publishers. 166–293.

Daston, Lorraine (2012). "The Sciences of the Archive." *Osiris* 27:1, 156–87.

Endress, Gerhard (1974). "Casimir Petraitis, *The Arabic version of Aristotle's* Meteorology" (review). *Oriens* 23/24, 497–509.

——— (1992). "Die wissenschaftliche Literatur," *Grundriss der arabischen Philologie*, vol. 3, ed. Wolfdietrich Fischer. Wiesbaden: Reichert. 3–152.

van Ess, Josef (1991–1997). *Theologie und Gesellschaft im 2. und 3. Jahrhundert Hidschra: Eine Geschichte des religiösen Denkens im frühen Islam*. Berlin: Walter de Gruyter. (6 vols.)

Fahd, Toufic (1995). "Sakīna." *Encyclopaedia of Islam*, 2nd ed. Vol. 8, 888–89.

Feliu, Lluís (2003). *The God Dagan in Bronze Age Syria*, tr. Wilfred G. E. Watson. Leiden and Boston: Brill. Series title: Culture and History of the Ancient Near East, vol. 19.

Foucault, Michel (1994). *The Order of Things*, [tr. Alan Sheridan]. New York: Vintage.

Gehlken, Erlend (2012). *Weather Omens of* Enūma Anu Enlil: *Thunderstorms, Wind and Rain (Tablets 44–99)*. Leiden: Brill. Series title: Cuneiform Monographs, vol. 43.

van Gelder, Geert Jan (1988). "'The Most Natural Poem of the Arabs': An Addition to the *Dīwān* of al-Kumayt ibn Zayd." *Journal of Arabic Literature* 19:2, 95–107.

Gruendler, Beatrice (2001). "Lightning and Memory in Poetic Fragments from the Muslim West." *Crisis and Memory in Islamic Societies*, ed. Angelika Neuwirth and Andreas Pflitsch. Würzburg and Beirut: Ergon Verlag. 435–52.

Hämeen-Anttila, Jaakko (2004/2005). "Al-Asmaʿī, Early Arabic Lexicography and *Kutub al-Farq*." *Zeitschrift für Geschichte der Arabisch-Islamischen Wissenschaften* 16. 141–8.

——— (2002). *Maqāma: History of a Genre*. Wiesbaden: Harrassowitz Verlag. Series title: Diskurse der Arabistik, vol. 5.

———, ed. (1996). *Minor Rağaz Collections: Materials for the Study of Rağaz Poetry III*. Helsinki: Finnish Oriental Society. Series title: Studia Orientalia, vol. 78.

Hammond, Marlé (2010). *Beyond Elegy: Classical Arabic Women's Poetry in Context*. Oxford: Oxford University Press. Series title: British Academy Postdoctoral Fellowship Monographs.

Heinrichs, Wolfhart (1995). "Ru'ba b. al-ʿAdjdjādj." *Encyclopaedia of Islam*, 2nd ed. Vol. 8, 577–78.

——— (2006). "Ta'abbaṭa Sharran, Goethe, Shākir," *Reflections on Reflections: Near Eastern writers reading literature, dedicated to Renate Jacobi*, ed. Angelika Neuwirth and Andreas Christian Islebe. Wiesbaden: Reichert Verlag. 191–252,

Hilālī, Khawla Taqī al-Dīn (1982). *Dirāsat lughawiyya fī arājiz Ru'ba wa-al-ʿAjjāj*. Baghdad: Dār al-Rashīd li-l-Nashr. (2 vols.)

Ḥusayn, Ṭāhā (1973–1974). *al-Majmūʿa al-kāmila li-mu'allafāt al-Duktūr Ṭāhā Ḥusayn*. Beirut: Dār al-Kitāb al-Lubnānī. (15 vols.)

Hussaini, A. S. (1967). "Uways al-Qaranī and the Uwaysī Ṣūfīs." *The Muslim World* 57:2, 103–13.

Hussein, Ali Ahmad (2009). *The Lightning-Scene in Ancient Arabic Poetry: Function, Narration and Idiosyncrasy in Pre-Islamic and Early Islamic Poetry*. Wiesbaden: Harrassowitz Verlag. Series title: Arabische Studien, vol. 3.

Jeffery, Arthur (2007). *The Foreign Vocabulary of the Qur'ān*. Leiden: Brill. Reprint.

Jumʿa, Fāṭima Amīn (1993). *Kitāb al-Maṭar li-Abī Zayd al-Anṣārī: Dirāsa lughawiyya*. Riyadh: King Saud University, Center for University Studies for Women.

Krupnik, Igor, and Ludger Müller-Wille (2010). "Franz Boas and Inuktitut Terminology for Ice and Snow: From the Emergence of the Field to the 'Great Eskimo Vocabulary Hoax.'" *SIKU: Knowing Our Ice: Documenting Inuit Sea Ice Knowledge and Use*, ed. Igor Krupnik et al. Dordrecht, Heidelberg, London and New York: Springer Verlag. 377–400.

Kunitzsch, Paul (1961). *Untersuchungen zur Sternnomenklatur der Araber*. Wiesbaden: Otto Harrassowitz.

Lane, Edward William (1863–1893). *An Arabic-English Lexicon*. London: Williams and Norgate; repr. Beirut: Librairie de Liban, 1968. (8 vols.)

Larcher, Pierre (2012). *Le brigand et l'amant: deux poèmes préislamiques de Ta'abbaṭa Sharran et Imru' al-Qays*. Paris: Sindbad.

Larsen, David (2015). "More Gravy than the Grave: Classical Arabic lexical monographs in translation." *postmedieval* 6: 127–35.

Larsen, David (2017). "Re-Introducing Wasnā bint ʿĀmir al-Asadiyya." *Dear Kathleen: Essays on the Occasion of Kathleen Fraser's 80th Birthday*, ed. Susan Gevirtz and Stephen Motika. New York: Nightboat Books. 27–32.

Le Roy Ladurie, Emmanuel (1988). *Times of Feast, Times of Famine: A History of Climate Since the Year 1000*, tr. Barbara Bray. New York: Farrar, Straus and Giroux.

Lecker, Michael (1997). "Zayd b. Thābit, 'A Jew With Two Sidelocks': Judaism and Literacy in Pre-Islamic Medina (Yathrib)." *Journal of Near Eastern Studies* 56:4, 259–73.

Lloyd, G. E. R. (1964). "The Hot and the Cold, the Dry and the Wet in Greek Philosophy." *Journal of Hellenic Studies* 84: 92–106.

MacDonald, M. C. A. (1992). "The Seasons and Transhumance in the Safaitic Inscriptions." *Journal of the Royal Asiatic Society* 2:1, 1–11.

Martin, Laura (1986). "'Eskimo Words for Snow': A Case Study in the Genesis and Decay of an Anthropological Example." *American Anthropologist* 88:2, 418–23.

Meissner, Bruno (1896). "Pallacottas." *Mitteilungen der Vorderasiatschen Gesellschaft* 1: 177–89.

Miller, Nathaniel A. (2024). *The Emergence of Arabic Poetry: From Regional Identities to Islamic Canonization*. Philadelphia: University of Pennsylvania Press.

——— (2017). "Seasonal Poetics: The Dry Season and Autumn Rains among Pre-Islamic Naǧdī and Ḥiǧāzī Tribes." *Arabica* 64:1, 1–27.

Mourad, Suleiman Ali (2006). *Early Islam between Myth and History: al-Ḥasan al-Baṣrī (d. 110H/728CE) and the Formation of His Legacy in Classical Islamic Scholarship*. Leiden and Boston: Brill.

Nie Minli (2016). "*Yin* and *Yang*, and the Hot and the Cold." *Frontiers of Philosophy in China* 11.1, 73–87.

Odhiambo, George O. (2017). "Water scarcity in the Arabian Peninsula and socio-economic implications." *Applied Water Science* 7:5, 2479–92.

Papoutsakis, Nefeli (2009). *Desert Travel as a Form of Boasting: A Study of Dū r-Rumma's Poetry*. Wiesbaden: Harrassowitz Verlag. Series title: Arabische Studien, vol. 4.

Pollock, Sheldon (2014). "Philology in three dimensions." *postmedieval* 5: 398–413.

Popper, William (1951). *The Cairo Nilometer: Studies in Ibn Taghrî Birdî's Chronicles of Egypt: I*. Berkeley and Los Angeles: University of California Press. Series title: University of California Publications in Semitic Philology, vol. 12.

al-Rājiḥī, ʿAbduh (1969). *al-Laḥajāt al-ʿarabiyya fī al-qirāʾāt al-Qurʾāniyya*. Cairo: Dār al-Maʿārif.

Rao, K. Koteswara, et al. (2024). "Future changes in the precipitation regime over the Arabian Peninsula with special emphasis on UAE: insights from NEX-GDDP CMIP6 model simulations." *Scientific Reports* 14:151.

Rapoport, Yossef and Emilie Savage-Smith, ed. and tr. (2014). *An Eleventh-Century Egyptian Guide to the Universe: the* Book of Curiosities [*Gharāʾib al-funūn wa-mulaḥ al-ʿuyūn*]. Leiden and Boston: Brill, 2014. Series title: Islamic Philosophy, Theology and Science, vol. 87.

Renaud, H. P. J. (1947). "L'origine du mot 'almanach.'" *Isis* 37:1/2, 44–46.

Rendsburg, Gary (1983). "Hebrew *RḤM* = 'Rain'." *Vetus Testamentum* 33:3, 357–62.

Renfroe, Fred (1992). *Arabic-Ugaritic Lexical Studies*. Munster: Ugarit-Verlag. Series title: Abhandlungen zur Literatur Alt-Syrien-Palästinas, vol. 5.

Rosenthal, Franz (1956). *Humor in Early Islam*. Leiden: Brill.

al-Sayyid, Ibrāhīm Yūsuf (1980). *Abū Zayd al-Anṣārī wa-atharuhu fī dirāsat al-lugha*. Riyadh: ʿImādat Shuʾūn al-Maktabāt, Jāmiʿat al-Riyāḍ.

Schimmel, Annemarie (1995). *Mystical Dimensions of Islam*. Chapel Hill: University of North Carolina Press.

Schoeler, Gregor (2009). *The Genesis of Literature in Islam: From the Aural to the Read*, tr. Shawkat Toorawa. Edinburgh: Edinburgh University Press. Series title: New Edinburgh Islamic Surveys.

——— (2006). *The Oral and the Written in Early Islam*, ed. James E. Montgomery, tr. Uwe Vagelpohl. London and New York: Routledge. Series title: Routledge Studies in Middle Eastern Literature.

Schub, Michael B. (1974). "A Note on the Dialect of Tamīm and Barth's Law." *Zeitschrift der Deutschen Morgenländischen Gesellschaft* 124:1, 13–14.

Sellheim, Rudolf (2002). "al-Yazīdī." *Encyclopaedia of Islam*, 2nd ed. Vol. 11, 316–17.

Serres, Michel (1982). *Hermes: Literature, Science, Philosophy*, ed. Josué V. Harari and David F. Bell. Baltimore: Johns Hopkins University Press.

Sersen, William John (1976). "Arab Meteorology: From Pre-Islamic Times to the Thirteenth Century A.D." Ph.D. dissertation, University of London.

al-Shak'a, Muṣṭafā (1991). *Manāhij al-ta'līf 'indā 'ulamā' al-'arab, qism al-adab*. Beirut: Dār al-'Ilm li-l-Malāyīn. 6th printing.

al-Shidyāq, Aḥmad Fāris (AH 1299 = 1880–1). *al-Jāsūs 'alā al-Qāmūs*. Constantinople: Maṭba'at al-Jawā'ib.

Sperl, Stefan, and Christopher Shackle, eds. (1996). *Qasida Poetry in Islamic Asia and Africa*. Leiden: Brill. (2 vols.)

Szombathy, Zoltan (2004). "Ridiculing the Learned: Jokes About the Scholarly Class in Mediaeval Arabic Literature." *Al-Qanṭara* 25:1, 93–117.

Tillier, Mathieu (2006). "Un traité politique du IIe/VIIIe siècle: L'epître de 'Ubayd Allāh b. al-Ḥasan al-'Anbarī au calife al-Mahdī." *Annales Islamologiques* 40: 139–70.

Turfa, Jean MacIntosh (2012). *Divining the Etruscan World: The Brontoscopic Calendar and Religious Practice*. New York: Cambridge University Press.

Tynianov, Yuri (1981). *The Problem of Verse Language*, ed. and tr. Michael Sosa and Brent Harvey. Ann Arbor: Ardis.

Varisco, Daniel M. (2017). "Pumping Yemen Dry: A History of Yemen's Water Crisis." *Human Ecology* 47:3, 317–29.

——— (1991). "The Origin of the *Anwā'* in Arab Tradition." *Studia Islamica* 74: 5–28.

——— (1987). "The Rain Periods in Pre-Islamic Arabia." *Arabica* 34:2, 251–66.

Versteegh, C. H. M. (1993). *Arabic Grammar and Qur'ānic Exegesis in Early Islam*. Leiden, New York and Cologne: Brill. Series title: Studies in Semitic Languages and Linguistics, vol. 19.

Wagner, Ewald (2010–2011). "Was Blitzt wo und warum bei Abū Nuwās?" *Quaderni di Studi Arabi*, Nuova Serie, 5/6: 89–102.

Weipert, Reinhard (2010). "Abū Zayd al-Anṣārī," *Encyclopaedia of Islam*, 3rd ed.

Wild, Stefan (1987). "Arabische Lexicographie." *Grundriss der arabischen Philologie*, vol. 2, ed. Helmut Gätje. Wiesbaden: Ludwig Reichert Verlag. 136–47.

Zakharia, Katia (1999). "Uways al-Qaranī: visages d'une légende." *Arabica* 46:2, 230–58.

Zwettler, Michael (1993). "Desert Yearning or Partisan Polemic? On the lines ascribed to Maysūn, wife of Muʿāwiya." *Asiatische Studien* 47:2, 299–372.